Moral Leadership

Moral Leadership

Integrity ✧ Courage ✧ Imagination

Robert Michael Franklin

ORBIS BOOKS
Maryknoll, New York 10545

Founded in 1970, Orbis Books endeavors to publish works that enlighten the mind, nourish the spirit, and challenge the conscience. The publishing arm of the Maryknoll Fathers and Brothers, Orbis seeks to explore the global dimensions of the Christian faith and mission, to invite dialogue with diverse cultures and religious traditions, and to serve the cause of reconciliation and peace. The books published reflect the views of their authors and do not represent the official position of the Maryknoll Society. To learn more about Maryknoll and Orbis Books, please visit our website at www.orbisbooks.com.

Manufactured in the United States of America.
Manuscript editing and typesetting by Joan Weber Laflamme.

Library of Congress Cataloging-in-Publication Data

Names: Franklin, Robert Michael, 1954– author.
Title: Moral leadership : integrity, courage, imagination / Robert Michael Franklin.
Description: Maryknoll, NY : Orbis Books, 2020. | Includes bibliographical references and index. | Summary: "A public intellectual and former president of Morehouse College offers reflections on the meaning of moral leadership"— Provided by publisher.
Identifiers: LCCN 2019042524 (print) | LCCN 2019042525 (ebook) | ISBN 9781626983588 (cloth) | ISBN 9781608338238 (ebook)
Subjects: LCSH: Leadership—Moral and ethical aspects.
Classification: LCC HD57.7 .F728 2020 (print) | LCC HD57.7 (ebook | DDC 174/.4—dc23
LC record available at https://lccn.loc.gov/2019042524
LC ebook record available at https://lccn.loc.gov/2019042525

In loving memory of

Lee Ethel Franklin and Cheryl Rachel Franklin,

and to the great cloud of witnesses past and present,
and those to come who will vindicate our hope.

Contents

Acknowledgments

Much of the material in this book was first presented as part of the Currie Lectures at Austin Seminary, Austin, Texas, in 2019. I am grateful to President Ted Wardlaw for the invitation to join what has been a long history in the city of Austin of gathering thought leaders to present important ideas. Much of the manuscript was drafted during a two-week extraordinary writers' retreat known as Mesa Refuge in Point Reyes, California, outside San Francisco. I shared those long, rich days of ideas with two amazing thought leaders, Dahlia Litwick, a writer and journalist at Slate and *Newsweek*, and Ramon Castellblanch, a health-policy expert and advocate in San Francisco. I am grateful to Dr. Chris Leighton, who introduced me to the Refuge and to its visionary founder, Peter Barnes, and the staff that is managed by a wise woman and great spirit, Susan Page Tillett.

In 2018, I delivered two eulogies. One for my sister, Cheri, and months later for my mother. Although we are all still recovering, my three brothers, David, Andrew, and Kwame, and their spouses, Monica, Sandra, and Charlotte, have been a source of renewal when I felt discouraged. My bedrock has been my dear wife and friend of over three decades, Cheryl Goffney. Cheryl has promoted social justice by seeking to eliminate and alleviate health disparities. My daughter, Imani, earned degrees in law and public administration and has worked to advance refugee rights and protect immigrants and women in the United States and Middle East. Robert M. Franklin, III, is teaching the world to think and feel through his literary gifts. And my oldest son, Julian M. DeShazier, is a pastor and vocal artist in Chicago, helping people to come alive in an important congregation in the heart of the University of Chicago campus and Hyde Park community. Julian and his wife, Mallory, have given us granddaughters, Dania Elle and Genevieve Lee, moral warriors of tomorrow. My extended family and friendship network has offered great encouragement over the years, especially Gladys R. Goffney, Tara R. Goffney, and Vicky L. DeShazier.

Living in Atlanta, I have been blessed with relationships and enjoyed unlimited access to many of America's civil rights movement pioneers and leaders. I spent valuable time with Rev. Martin Luther King Sr., Mrs. Coretta Scott King, and all four of her children; Rev. Ralph David Abernathy Sr. and Mrs. Juanita Abernathy; Rev. Hosea Williams; Donald Hollowell; Dr. Asa Yancey Sr.; Dr. Hamilton Holmes; Bernard Lafayette; Dr. C. T. Vivian; and Rev. James Orange. I am grateful to Ambassador Andrew Young, Congressman John Lewis, and Rev. Joseph Lowery, who continue to inspire while avoiding the 'great man' syndrome.

Many friends and colleagues at Candler School of Theology and the Center for the Study of Law and Religion, Emory Law School informed my thinking and many read parts of the manuscript. I am grateful to my extraordinary Laney Program colleague and friend Dr. Letitia Campbell and the Laney Program associates who have advanced our efforts to educate moral leaders; these associates include Richard Landers, Allison Henderson-Brooks, and Kiya Ward. Emory's visionary president, Claire E. Sterk, and provost, Dwight A. McBride, have been enormously helpful in fostering a collegial environment for focusing on the role of the university as a moral leader.

Other colleagues from Morehouse College discussed or read parts of the manuscript and offered valuable insight. They include Dillard University President Emeritus Dr. Samuel DuBois Cook and Mrs. Sylvia Cook; Morehouse President David Thomas; Rev. Amos Brown; Lawrence E. Carter, dean of the Martin Luther King Jr. International Chapel; the late Willie "Flash" Davis and Robert C. Davidson, board chairmen; Dr. Vicki Crawford, director of the Morehouse College Martin Luther King Jr. Papers; college historian Dr. Marcellus Barksdale; and Derek Alphran. I am indebted to Henry Louis Gates and Cornel West for their encouragement throughout the process, along with conversation partners Peter J. Paris, Cheryl Townsend Gilkes, Walter E. Fluker, and former Dekalb County executive Burrell Ellis. Documentary filmmaker Martin Doblmeier has offered wise counsel over the years, and Collie Burnett of the Atlanta Interfaith Broadcast challenged me to think about innovative and multimedia ways of disseminating my ideas.

Following my retirement from Morehouse, we were blessed to reside in California. It was gratifying to learn from and work with the California Endowment and President Robert K. Ross, Angela Glover Blackwell at PolicyLink, and Los Angeles County Supervisor Mark Ridley-Thomas, who organized leadership roundtables and presentations on moral leadership among at-risk young people throughout the state of California. My sabbatical was spent at Stanford University at the Martin Luther King Jr. Research and Education Institute, where Clayborne Carson was a wonderful host, teacher, and conversation partner. I learned much from conversations with Emmett Carson at the Silicon Valley Community Foundation, Bishop Jerry W. Macklin in Hayward, Rev. Michael McBride in Oakland, Dr. J. Alfred Smith Sr., Rev. Claybon Lea Jr., and Clemmie and Rosiland T. Roberts, who introduced me to community leaders in Northern California.

We were thrilled to return to Atlanta at the invitation of Candler School of Theology Dean Jan Love. She and Associate Dean Jonathan Strom have provided constant support of our work in the James T. and Berta R. Laney Legacy in Moral Leadership Program at Candler School of Theology. Ralph Smith, Carol Thompson, and Joy Moore at the Annie E. Casey Foundation have been longstanding conversation partners who have taught me more than I can express. Senior leaders at the Ford Foundation, including Franklin A. Thomas, Susan Berresford, Alison Bernstein, Melvin Oliver, and Darren Walker provided wonderful examples of courageous thinking and strategic investing in promising program ideas.

William Lewis and Carol Sutton Lewis supported my efforts to meet, interview, and gather information on moral leadership across cultures serving young men of color. They have a mission to connect a national network of leaders who are committed to an inclusive democracy that works for all. Vernon Jordan, Michael Lomax, former governor Deval Patrick, and the Martha's Vineyard community were attentive and challenging conversation partners. And the Atlanta Business League and Leona Barr Davenport offered early support to enable inquiries into organizations with strong cultures that prioritize fostering moral agency and leadership development. I am also grateful for the insights into the evolving and volatile world of business attained through conversations and working together on community enhancement projects with Richard H. Anderson, former CEO of Delta Air Lines; Arthur M. Blank, cofounder of Home Depot and owner of the Atlanta Falcons football team; Muhtar Kent, former chairman and CEO of Coca-Cola; Dan and S. Truett Cathy of Chick-fil-A; and Tom Becker and Michael Hill of the Chautauqua Institution.

I am grateful for the support of our church families in Chicago, founded by Bishop Louis H. Ford of the St. Paul Church of God in Christ (COGIC); in Atlanta, with Rev. Dr. Raphael Warnock and the Ebenezer Baptist Church, and Dr. Jonathan Greer of the Cathedral of Faith Church; and in California with Bishop Charles and Mae Blake of West Angeles COGIC, our West Coast pastor and friends. I am forever indebted to Dr. James T. and Berta R. Laney for their encouragement, inspiration, and friendship of many years. A special word of appreciation goes to Trent Frank, my former student and assistant, who assisted with several items in the final stages of preparing the manuscript. Finally, I was guided and encouraged by the wise and discerning advice of Robert Ellsberg, publisher and editor-in-chief at Orbis Books.

There is so much more to see and do, and miles to go before any of us should sleep.

Preface

I wish I knew how
It would feel to be free
I wish I could break
All the chains holding me
I wish I could say
All the things that I should say
Say 'em loud say 'em clear
For the whole 'round world to hear

I wish I could share
All the love that's in my heart
Remove all the bars
That keep us apart
I wish you could know
What it means to be me
Then you'd see and agree
That every man should be free

I wish I could give
All I'm longin' to give
I wish I could live
Like I'm longin' to live
I wish I could do
All the things that I can do
And though I'm way over due
I'd be startin' anew

—Nina Simone
(lyrics by Billy Taylor)

I came of age on the South Side of Chicago during the 1960s. Part of the soundtrack of those years was provided by Nina Simone singing "I Wish I Knew How It Would Feel to Be Free." It was an exhilarating, volatile period. You may be aware of the stories about the great refugee migration of rural southern African Americans that often unfolded in two stages: first, from the rural south to the urban south, and in many cases, a second move from the urban south to the urban north. My family was part of what has been described as the largest migration in such a short concentration of years in American history. We migrated from Mississippi to West Memphis, Arkansas, then north to Chicago to escape the domestic terrorism of lynching and to pursue greater economic and personal development opportunities. But, there was a shadowy side to our life in the city. The street gangs of Chicago were already world famous.

One day, two groups of young men gathered on the street directly in front of my grandmother's house. We lived with my grandmother for many years until my parents could save a down payment to purchase a larger home where she moved in with us. The boys were arguing about something and preparing to fight. All of a sudden, out of nowhere, my grandmother ran from her kitchen through the house, onto the front porch, down the stairs, with apron flying in the wind, and right into the street to place her body between these muscle-bound young men. I was eight or nine years old and horrified that she was putting my reputation on the line this way. But I listened. She spoke to both groups of boys and said, "No one is fighting here today. I know what it's like for a mother to get a phone call that her son has been shot. My son was shot in Europe in World War II. I have fed many of your families from that little garden next door. I know your mothers. Your mothers don't want to get that call." It was an incredible scene.

I watched these tough homeboys look at her, look at each other, look at her, look at their friends, and begin to back away. No words spoken. She placed her body and authority between them, backing them off and disrupting the usual flow of street brawls. They disbanded, certain to fight another day. No other mothers or fathers intervened like that, although a few watched timidly from their porches. But because of this one woman and her moral courage and imagination, there would be no fight that day in that place. I am writing because I must bear witness to the life of Mother Martha Battle McCann from Battle, Mississippi.

Most books on moral leadership are written by scholars on the topic and do not see light beyond the edge of a university campus or a congregational parking lot. Unfortunately, many people are unaware that important conversations about moral leadership are happening inside the community's anchor institutions. More important, beyond the conversations, these enduring community institutions are doing the hard work of nurturing and producing moral leaders—sometimes as simple as grandmothers mentoring and modeling leadership for the kids around them; sometimes more formal and text centered.

Given the state of our polarized nation and world, the topic of moral leadership is open and awaiting participants. Years after my grandmother passed away, I reflected on her unusual gifts of hospitality, care, and discipline. Through them, I realized that she was extending an invitation, hoping that I, that we, would respond by loving the things that she loved, caring for the people for whom she cared. This preface is dedicated to her and to your grandmother and all of the other change agents and moral leaders who have given us a pretty good world. Now, it's up to us to improve it.

My grandmother was not there when I graduated from Morehouse in 1975, nor was she there in 2007 when I became the tenth president of the college. But I thought about her the morning that I was to be introduced to a commencement audience during the final commencement of my predecessor and distinguished physicist Dr. Walter E. Massey. My story affirms the deep affection of the national community for Morehouse as an enduring institution that merits the confidence of some of the nation's most influential citizens. Indeed, many of them encourage their sons to attend with hopes that they will in the course of education become moral agents and leaders.

Just before the procession, platform guests gathered to don their robes and take photos, all except two people, the actor Denzel Washington and me. Apparently we were acting out of habit rather than following the memo. We went to the president's office instead of the student center. One of the college staff was on hand to lead us across campus just in time to robe and join the lines. As we walked and talked, he expressed pride in his son's recent graduation from Morehouse, a young man who went on to become a Golden Globes–nominated actor and artist. I felt the pride in the tradition and legacy of this village asset that occupies a unique place in the hearts of people.

We hurriedly walked outside on a gorgeous Sunday morning to the sight of thousands of people on the stunningly beautiful and stately college yard, the same yard where Dr. Martin Luther King Jr.'s funeral and memorial service occurred on April 9, 1968, as tens of thousands gathered and millions watched from afar. Sitting in our living room in Chicago, I was part of that TV audience, and I became entranced with this place, and with President Benjamin Mays, who delivered the amazing eulogy that day. As we began to walk through the parted Red Sea of an excited audience, I realized that processing in front of me were filmmaker Spike Lee and actor Wesley Snipes. Behind me were Denzel and a famous boxing promoter, Butch Lewis. As we processed, people were going crazy, with deafening noise and shouts, snapping photos, calling out to these national celebrities, and enjoying the moment. I felt like the potted plant in this company. But, I knew that in a few days, after the masses had dispersed with their graduates, I would be responsible for steering this great ship and setting the tone for our future. It felt like an object lesson on stewardship and leadership. I had an important role to play, I had authority and power, but I was at once the least interesting and most ignored person in the picture. I smiled. What a metaphor for how authentic leadership works.

That's when I heard my grandmother whisper: "Work hard, be sincere, change lives on a daily basis, and you may or may not be noticed. But, never forget that your work is undeniably important. The things that people take for granted and in which they have great pride are on your shoulders. Be faithful. March forward."

Introduction

Every saint has a past, every sinner has a future.

—OSCAR WILDE

A few years ago, while attending the 100th anniversary of Emory University's School of Law, my wife and I stood in a crowded gymnasium at a reception awaiting the moment when the doors would open for the banquet. While standing there, nursing a glass of club soda and lime, a law professor greeted me. We chatted, and I learned about his academic interests. Then he asked what I do. I noted that I am a professor in moral leadership who explores the zone where ethics and leadership studies overlap. His first reaction was amusing, "Moral leadership, is that a thing?" I could have returned with a cheap-shot joke, such as, "Among lawyers, perhaps not so much." But I refrained.

He listened intently as I explained that this topic or area of study is concerned with the intersection between leadership studies and ethics. That is where longstanding theoretical and practical questions about effective leadership encounter the theory and practice of the good life and the just society. He was suddenly intrigued. "Well, that should be taught immediately on Capitol Hill," he said.

Later, I reflected that what this colleague had quickly surmised was not only that moral leadership is a thing, but that it might actually be a welcome response to an urgent public and private need.

I maintain that throughout history, when human communities have faced seemingly insurmountable challenges, women and men with integrity, courage, and imagination have emerged to help lead them forward. Sociologist Robert N. Bellah speaks of this phenomenon:

> In times of national difficulty, when the existing order of things appears unequal to its challenges, Americans have often sought new visions of social life. But when new visions have appeared, they typically have done so not through political parties, as in many European societies, but in the form of social movements . . . from Abolition to Prohibition, from organized labor to Civil Rights.[1]

This book has a very practical goal: to stimulate conversations about the nature of moral leadership and why we need more of it now. There are several reasons why this is the case.

First, democracy requires virtue. Nearly all of the founders of this country believed this. They maintained, furthermore, that citizens have a right to insist upon the moral behavior of their leaders. America, as a new republic, was born and nurtured in the incubator of virtue. This is our debt to John Adams, Abigail Adams, Abraham Lincoln, Frederick Douglass, Ida B. Wells, Eleanor Roosevelt, and many others. Democracy requires virtue. And most of the time we have found it. As Secretary of State William Seward said during the Civil War: "There is always just enough virtue in this republic to save it; sometimes none to spare, but still enough to meet the emergency."

Second, as most people would agree, we are now in a state of steady moral decline—almost a nosedive. David Crary of the Associated Press puts it this way: "Public cynicism about America's moral standards is high, as evidenced in the annual Values and Morals poll

---

[1] Robert Neelly Bellah, et al., *Habits of the Heart: Individualism and Commitment in American Life* (Oakland: University of California Press, 1985), 212.

conducted by Gallup since 2002. In the latest poll, released last June, a record high 49 percent of respondents rated moral values in the U.S. as poor, and only 14 percent rated them excellent or good."[2] We need the virtue conversation because we are slipping; we are losing ethical ground.

Third, moral decline can be contagious. These trend lines of lying, cheating, theft, hatred, violence, racism, Islamophobia, homophobia, transphobia, and so on will not suddenly stop and reverse themselves. According to Andrew Cullison, a philosophy professor who leads DePauw University's Prindle Institute for Ethics, "The perception that unethical behavior is increasingly commonplace could have a snowball effect. People think that if moral standards have eroded, why should they play by the rules. If they've lost trust in some entity or institution, then that organization has lost the right to their compliance with the rules."[3] The recent admissions-for-sale scandal in certain colleges and universities is an example that calls for a serious response. The corrosive effects of an attitude that prizes deception and winning at all costs can leave those who play by the rules thinking they need to come up with their own way of gaming the system.

Fourth, the contagion can be deadly. This moral decline threatens to destroy our families, schools, congregations, communities, and our very nation, but it will also bore into individual human souls, emptying or hollowing out that part of us that can appreciate and recognize what is good, true, and beautiful. We will become rotten people. We will not fund the education of children who do not look like our own. We will resist acknowledging our unconscious biases. We will become numb to offenses, private and public. When the president of the United States behaves badly, we will sigh in resignation. We will learn to make peace with evil. What else can we do?

---

[2] David Crary, Associated Press, "Admissions Scandal Unfolds amid Cynicism about Moral Values," March 15, 2019.

[3] Andew Cullison, in Crary, "Admissions Scandal Unfolds."

Professor Cullison observes, "It's the objective truth that norms of conduct are being violated. . . . Where people differ is how outraged they are. If you're getting what you want (in terms of policy), you'll be more willing to look the other way."[4]

Jordan Libowitz, a spokesman for the watchdog group Citizens for Responsibility and Ethics in Washington, notes that a number of President Trump's cabinet appointees have been the subject of ethics investigations. He says: "We're seeing a pattern of not caring about ethics that we've not seen before. . . . It sets a dangerous precedent for future administrations, that once ethical norms are pushed aside and nothing is done about it, this might become the new normal."[5]

To those who are skeptical about the topic or study of leadership, let me begin by saying I share your skepticism, even disdain, for hypocritical leaders, for demagogues, con men, and other despicable manipulators of public trust. But does that mean that all leaders are the same? Do the traits, values, and behaviors of the leader matter? Are leaders fungible? Do they make a difference?

Obviously, I believe that leadership matters. Pick an issue, any social problem, and think about the many interventions one could make: passing a law, investing money, donating money, increasing or decreasing regulations, threatening punishment, creating incentives, changing the brands and messages. . . . All of these have a role in effecting social and personal change. I would argue that, regardless of the issue, the addition of one or two moral leaders to the equation dramatically transforms the situation, and may or should do so in ways that bring long-term and sustainable social goods. The goods that leaders create and cultivate include a sense of community, social trust, nondiscrimination, shared prosperity, equal justice, hope, friendship, and the willingness to make sacrifices for strangers. Those are lofty ideals, and it is a bold claim that moral leaders can help to unleash these possibilities, but I believe that to be the case. Throughout this book I profile people who have done just that.

---

[4] Ibid.

[5] Jordan Libowitz, in Crary, ""Admission Scandal Unfolds."

In short, my argument is that good leadership matters, and moral leadership matters more.

In the mid-nineteenth century Alexis de Tocqueville wrote: "The greatness of America lies not in being more enlightened than any other nation, but rather in her ability to repair her faults."[6] In this country, perhaps in every country, nations and peoples have exhibited respect for leaders who have helped to heal and repair national faults.

I think that it matters where one begins the conversation about revitalizing the health of a democracy and its possibilities of creating a just and good society. When we expand our focus beyond ideas for repairing our society to the purveyor of those ideas, then we are dealing with the topic of leadership, and at that point different foci come into view. For instance, we might wish to know something about the personal qualities, traits, vices, and virtues of leaders. Do they appear to be generous or selfish, wise or foolish, patient or rash? We might be curious to know how they think, how they reason through an issue, problem, or crisis. We might want to know what they have done in the past, and what they would do in the future. Thoughts and deeds matter. I think we might also want to know what impact leaders have made and promise to make in the future. What impacts are possible for leaders to make?

I have chosen to divide my reflections into three distinct but interrelated questions: First, who are these moral leaders and how do they come to be such? Second, what and how do they think and act? And, third, what impacts do moral leaders have or enable?

America has strong roots in Anglo-European-African-Indigenous-Latinx symbols and culture. But from the beginning, as historians have agreed, this young nation drew from two principal sources to inform and shape its identity, purpose, and destiny in the larger world. These were, of course, the Bible and the Enlightenment tradition. The Bible taught Americans to speak of the

---

[6] Alexis de Tocqueville, *Democracy in America* (Chicago: University of Chicago Press, 2002).

individual value and worth (sanctity or sacredness of the human soul) of every person. It invited people to trust that the order in the universe reflected divine intention. At the same time, the rational, skeptical, and philosophical elements of the Enlightenment tradition taught Americans to question authority and to demand that political and social systems be justified on rational grounds. Some interpretations and applications of biblical revelation were employed to justify the divine right of kings, slavery, and the subjugation of women. The Enlightenment tradition challenged these assertions and usually demanded the highest respect for personal freedom and dignity.

On that basis it seems appropriate to speak of moral leadership that is inclusive of all religious beliefs and motivations but is also independent of revelation and faith. Morality can be justified on the basis of right reason. Faith, whether Christian, Muslim, Jewish, Hindu, Buddhist, or other, provides important guidance and inspiration to uphold the moral good.

I am and aspire to be a Christian leader, and I believe in the authenticity and power of public Christian witness. Augustine, Aquinas, Martin Luther, William Wilberforce, Richard Allen, Harriet Tubman, Martin Luther King Jr., and Dorothy Day demonstrate that distinctively Christian public moral leadership has been and can be a history-changing vocation—and one to which more Christian leaders should aspire. As G. K. Chesterton writes, "The Christian faith hasn't been tried and found wanting. It has been found difficult and left untried."[7] Nevertheless, we know that this nation and the world are better today thanks to the sacrifice, struggle, and leadership of many non-Christians. We have gladly received the leadership gifts of Rabbi Abraham Joshua Heschel, Mahatma Gandhi, His Holiness the Dalai Lama, and Muhammad Ali.

In our radically diverse society we need ways to communicate with fellow citizens who do not share our theological convictions. Even approaches to truth, justice, and goodness may be found in

---

[7] G. K. Chesterton, *What's Wrong with the World* (New York: Sheed and Ward, 1956).

approaches that are not religious at all. Some are even skeptical and critical of religion. That, too, is a gift. Enlightenment traditions can help us to get to where we all want to go because religions have proven themselves to be capable of so much injustice, violence, ignorance, and abuse of power that they need to be held accountable by the authority of reason, logic, and common sense. This was indelibly imprinted a few months after the 9/11 tragedy. I visited Ground Zero in New York City, and while walking near the smoldering and pungent site, I saw on a wooden panel in the fence that someone had written, "God, save us from your followers!"

Religions need reason. But reason also needs to be kept accountable for its more insidious capacity to oppress. Reason as philosophical, secular, rational discourse about truth, goodness, justice, and beauty is clearly admirable. But reason can also be used to justify and legitimate injustice. Critiquing or reexamining traditions does not dismiss or disrespect them. Reason in history is good. The question is, how can we make it better?

In the first chapter I consider the process of identity formation of moral leaders. I set forth a definition of moral leadership that is inclusive of, but distinct from, moral agency. *Not all moral agents are leaders, but all moral leaders are first of all moral agents.* Moral agents are people who act in accord with their most deeply held values, principles, and beliefs about what is right, true, good, and beautiful. Such moral agency is a necessary foundation for moral leadership. But *moral leadership* involves something more. I define *moral leaders to be people who live and lead with integrity, courage, and imagination as they serve the common good, while inviting others to join them.* They are moral agents who respond to the vocation of leadership, which leads to the increase of righteousness, truth, goodness, and beauty—in other words, the enhancement of the common good. And they seek to expand this project or movement by enlisting others.

Many factors and experiences go into the development and making of moral leaders. It is interesting to think about how and why they become moral leaders, and what they actually think and do in the world. How did my grandmother become "that" person? We know what she did, what she could do, but what did she think about? From what she said that day, and from what I observed over the course of our life together, I know that she had a keen sense of the way God wanted the world—her world—to be ordered. And so that church lady went into the streets to make it happen.

The question of what moral leaders think and do is the focus of the second chapter. I suggest five behaviors or habits that are common among moral leaders. These behaviors or habits can and should be cultivated in those who aspire to lead.

Being identified as a moral agent or leader ultimately hinges on the judgment of others. It involves the retrospective assessment of *words spoken, lives lived, and deeds done.* The larger community of human observers makes the judgment about whether another person was or is a moral leader. That seems natural and appropriate, since leadership is a social act, one that implies a social contract among people. Among the normative actions of leaders is the commitment to building enduring institutions and movements that sustain their visions by fostering the development of other moral agents. That is the focus of the third chapter.

In reflecting on the impact that moral leaders can have and the difference they make through institutions, I reflect on my experience as a senior leader in two iconic American institutions: Morehouse College and Chautauqua Institution.

I conclude by highlighting efforts to heal our divided nation and repair frayed social bonds. Creating a just society and enabling good lives for all is an exciting, noble moral project. I believe that it requires moral leaders. My hope, for those who read these pages, is that something here will guide, unleash, and inspire your own capacity for moral leadership.

1

On Becoming Moral Agents
and Moral Leaders

*Be not afraid of greatness. Some are born
great, some achieve greatness, and some have
greatness thrust upon 'em.*

—Shakespeare, "Twelfth Night"

*People are trapped in history and history is
trapped in them.*

—James Baldwin

Strong people don't need strong leaders.

—Ella Baker

An author brings many hopes to a book. I hope that this book will invite readers to strive to be open, available, and willing to act as moral agents. I hope that many, maybe even most moral agents will also become moral leaders, people who habitually think through issues morally, then step forward to act, inviting and persuading others to join the movement for good. Elevating the focus beyond individual agency, I also hope organizations and institutions of all kinds will act courageously on behalf of the common good. As a former institutional president, I know that organizations can set the tone for an entire community's disposition. And the leaders of those institutions can set the tone for their institutions. This book is for both ordinary people and leaders. All of us may be just a few heartbeats and moments from becoming extraordinary.

I am especially hopeful that community-based organizations, colleges, and universities, houses of worship, and small businesses—those that are responsible for educating people and forming character—will pay attention to this book. I hope that many will devote more attention to the topic of moral agency and leadership. Like the law professor at the reception mentioned in the introduction, some might wonder if moral leadership is a thing. And if so, what does it have to do with the work of engineers, nurses, biologists, neuroscientists, entrepreneurs, accountants, artists, computer scientists, or lawyers? Why would a section on moral leadership appear in a textbook, newsletter, or syllabus for these various vocations? The topic of moral leadership may seem presumptuous, even audacious, but any human activity or practice that pertains to the betterment of the human community is appropriate for all of us to entertain.

Sometimes conversations about ethics are prompted by scandals or crises: government corruption after Watergate; corporate malfeasance at Enron; sexual harassment in the office place; sexual abuse among clergy, coaches, and other trusted authorities; police violence; and on and on.

Each of these crises prompted calls for new regulations or procedures for monitoring behavior or for setting penalties. Institutional leaders were forced to take more seriously than before the necessity of setting the tone at the top. Much of the focus in these cases was on risk management, mitigating damage to the brand, compliance, training, and monitoring. Few organizations invited and inspired employees and community members to aspire higher to active moral agency and leadership.

I believe that we may be entering a new era in which moral leadership is expected to repair broken trust and a frayed social contract. The work of authentic moral restoration will require a new institutional ethos guided by more thoughtful leaders who possess the integrity, courage, and imagination to lead this change. It is now time for all institutions in a democracy (the people's deliberative community)—government, companies, universities, houses of worship, arts institutions, and philanthropic organizations—to recognize that when they participate in social evil or behave badly, they have compromised public trust and must take the steps necessary for moral repair.

Against the backdrop of moral indifference and relativism, authentic moral leadership calls attention to itself. When there is a lack of moral leadership in an organization, it can emerge from unlikely places and people, often from the young. Villages have elders, and traditionally the elders lead. But it is particularly exciting to observe younger people, new to the burdens of sustaining fragile social life, aspire to contribute and add value to the best of their communities. Think of the high school students of Marjory Stoneman Douglass in Parkland, Florida, who stepped forward following the mass shooting in their school, when the moment called for bold leadership. As students, they were not trained to provide public moral leadership. And yet, after the public trauma in their community, an event that should have shocked their elders into action, it was instead the students who mobilized to affect the public conversation and to raise the bar of public morality and decency. The elders did not do that.

Harvard psychiatrist Robert Coles shed light on the rise of young leaders as he spoke of his teacher, Erik H. Erikson. Dr. Erikson, a legendary developmental psychoanalyst, often "spoke of the leadership that young people can provide to their elders, their parents and teachers. Courage is leadership affirmed."[1] The students of Marjory Stoneman Douglas High School and leaders of the Black Lives Matter movement are showing us something important. Ordinary citizens, especially young people, can refuse to accept the

---

[1] Robert Coles, *Lives of Moral Leadership: Men and Women Who Have Made a Difference* (New York: Random House, 2001), xxi.

usual political and "common sense" reasons for why law, policy, and behavioral change cannot or will not happen. They are demanding change. They are demonstrating strategic insight, patience, determination, and hope that the public can be persuaded to yearn for a different and better status quo. They are recalling Martin Luther King Jr.'s declaration: "If our world is to be saved from its impending doom it will come not through the complacent adjustment of the conforming majority but through the creative maladjustment of a nonconforming minority."[2] King went on to name Ralph Waldo Emerson and the biblical prophets as creatively maladjusted to social systems that produce and perpetuate injustice and oppression. One could say that youth are natural-born nonconformists.

The presence of older moral leaders who are inviting and mentoring the next generation of moral agents and leaders is a promising sign of community health. It signifies that someone is thinking about and holding firm to a community's highest aspiration, to transmit and preserve the best of its values and purpose to the next generation. Intergenerational mentoring is a testament to adults whom Erikson called "generative" people. How might all of our communities be improved if all adults did more to cultivate the values of civility, good character, generosity, and kindness?

Because we think of leaders as people who make a positive impact, most organizations devote attention to improving the quality of leadership. Different sectors tend to focus on the skill sets that are most relevant to their purposes. To business and military leaders we emphasize and promote the importance of strategic leadership. To nonprofit and faith leaders we teach servant leadership. But at a time when the bonds that connect us as Americans are unraveling, why are we not promoting moral leadership?

---

[2] In Clayborne Carson, Susan Carson, Susan Englander, Troy Jackson, and Gerald L. Smith, eds., *The Papers of Martin Luther King, Jr., Volume VI, Advocate of the Social Gospel, September 1948–March 1963* (Berkeley and Los Angeles: University of California Press, 2007).

Apart from the university or school, this topic also has important implications for families, our primary socializing institutions. Parenting, after all, is a form of moral leadership. The ancient Greeks understood that the household was the first classroom on virtue. Parents were expected to model, teach, and encourage the development of virtue. But those without children who seek to be better friends in covenantal relationship are also engaged in a moral enterprise. It is in this zone of care and discipline, which some religious traditions prefer to speak of as a sacrament, that human beings become better at being human.

This is a time when we all need to think about solutions to threats to our republic. Americans are passing through a complicated time in this nation's history, a time marked by intellectual and moral chaos and rancor. During such times we need to have conversations about how we will go forward together, guided by a reliable moral compass. In the past, people like Abraham Lincoln, Frederick Douglass, Eleanor Roosevelt, and Rosa Parks helped us to choose a better path forward. There are people like that around today, though they may not even realize it yet. But the constellation of circumstances, visions, and impulses to serve and lead can emerge unexpectedly and produce unpredictable results. Moral agency can spring forth spontaneously. As moral agents persist and continue to live in that mode, habits can form and moral leadership may be the result. This is the *telos* or end of a good person who is urgently concerned about others.

I hope that readers will examine the social and moral crises that face us now (partisan division; racial, gender, and class tensions; the role of guns in our society; immigration policy; the well-being of our children and youth; culture wars over the future of families; and more) and think about the most courageous and impactful course of action their ethical and religious values can underwrite. This highlights the ultimate adventure that should confront every moral agent every day. This constitutes the agenda for what moral agents and leaders are called to be and do in this immediate context.

Three Defining Virtues:
Centering Down, Stepping Forward, and Dreaming Up

My working definition of moral leadership has three key elements: (1) *people with integrity, courage, and imagination,* (2) *who serve the common good,* (3) *while inviting others to join them.*

I begin by prioritizing three virtues: integrity, courage, and imagination. There are many other virtues that are essential for moral leadership. One thinks of the classical virtues of prudence, temperance, courage, and justice. And then there are the theological virtues of faith, hope, and love. But I would place integrity, courage, and imagination at the center of attention for this moment in history when *integrity* and authenticity are necessary for restoring public trust, *courage* is required for defying the force of complacency, and *imagination* is essential for fashioning innovative responses to persistent problems, reframing familiar questions, and asking altogether new questions.

I see a parallel between the way some ancient thinkers prioritized liberal learning, beginning with the trivium of grammar, logic, and rhetoric. Mastery of those three topics did not conclude their learning agenda; it was foundational for what would follow. Thereafter students would be guided into the quadrivium: arithmetic, geometry, music, and astronomy. All seven (and more) areas of study were important, but some topics were prerequisites, providing a sense of order, proportion, and perspective for subsequent learning. In my thinking, *integrity, courage,* and *imagination* unfold and manifest according to their own distinctive rhythms.

Integrity: Centering Down

I see integrity as the art of *centering down* with intense focus on our most deeply held values, which then radiate outward in our behavior and demeanor. The great Christian mystic Howard Thurman spoke of centering down as a clarifying discipline that offers direction from a deep moral compass. I think of the image of a compass face that is submerged underwater. If the waters are calm, one can peer through them to read the compass. But if our lives contain waves and turbulence, we may see the compass and know it is there but be unable to discern locations in any precise manner. Centering is also calming and focusing. Sometimes, Dr. Thurman spoke of "listening for the sound of the genuine" in ourselves and in others. At a commencement address at Spelman College in 1981 he told students, "There is something in every one of you that waits and listens for the sound of the genuine in yourself. It is the only true guide you will ever have. And if you cannot hear it, you will all of your life spend your days on the ends of strings that somebody else pulls."

Integrity is the quality of wholeness and the seamless integration of values, intentions and behavior. Integrity is the starting place of all moral existence. Without integrity, action is untrustworthy and meaningless, and authentic leadership is impossible.

In his insightful book *Integrity*, Stephen L. Carter highlights two dimensions of the word as elaborated in the Oxford English Dictionary definition—completeness and perfection. Integrity is both "the condition of having no part or element taken away or wanting: undivided or unbroken state; material wholeness, completeness, entirety," and also "the condition of not being marred or violated; unimpaired or uncorrupted condition; original perfect state; soundness."[3] I maintain that it is also intimately related to and manifest in the virtue of courage, because every day we are subject to forces that do not respect our integrity, invite distraction, and offer fraudulent or false goals of need satisfaction.

Courage: Stepping Forward

I think of courage as the fearless activation of one's deepest convictions. As C. S. Lewis puts it, "Courage is not simply one of the virtues, but the form of every virtue at the testing point. A chastity

---

[3] Stephen L. Carter, *Integrity* (New York: Harper Perennial, 1996), 17.

or honesty, or mercy, which yields to danger will be chaste or honest or merciful only on conditions."[4] Courage, sometimes interpreted as fortitude, is one of the cardinal virtues in ancient moral philosophy along with temperance, prudence, and justice. It is interesting that the word *cardinal* is derived from the Latin word for "hinge." For many classical Christian thinkers, like Augustine and Aquinas, these four hinge virtues were combined with the theological virtues of faith, hope, and love to produce an enduring vision of the moral life.

The root of the word *courage* is *cor*, the Latin word for "heart." In an early form *courage* meant "to speak one's mind by telling all one's heart" or "telling the story of who you are with your whole heart."[5] Later, *courage* came to be understood as the ability to do dangerous things, to step forth for seemingly impossible tasks. No wonder we reserve the title (as a social good) of hero and heroine for those who step or leap forward to do good that others won't do.

Courage is the art of *stepping forward*. When others step back in the face of crisis, moral leaders step forward, make themselves available, accept the risk of standing alone when necessary, but are poised to act in an impactful way. Although the struggle for social justice is a "team sport," when Rosa Parks engaged in civil disobedience, she sat alone. She knew that she had allies and possibly a movement behind her, but that day she was alone.

When Martin Luther King Jr. and Ralph Abernathy led a dangerous march on the streets of Birmingham, surrounded by uncertain followers, they knelt on the sidewalk to pray, thereby sanctifying public space, and then they began to walk forward. Without looking over his shoulder, King whispered anxiously to Abernathy, "Ralph, are they coming? Are they following?" He hadn't checked to see if anyone was following before stepping forward.

---

[4] C. S. Lewis, *The Screwtape Letters* (London: Fontana Books, 1955), 148–49.

[5] Brene Brown, "The Power of Vulnerability," TED Talk (YouTube), January 3, 2011.

Imagination: Dreaming Up

Finally, imagination is the art of *dreaming up* where and how we can transcend the status quo. There is no more compelling trope of American dreaming than the dream that Martin Luther King Jr. shared on August 28, 1963. Those familiar with the history of that speech know that he had not planned to deliver those words for the climax of the speech. His text read differently. Before writing his speech, according to Clarence Jones, one of his key advisers, King had solicited ideas for its content. The opening of the speech spoke of America lacking sufficient funds to cash the promissory note of freedom and equality for all, an idea that Jones suggested. Clayborne Carson notes that "King had been drawing on material he used in the 'I Have a Dream' speech in his other speeches and sermons for many years."[6] Two months earlier, June 23, 1963, he had proclaimed most of the famous words we know in a meeting in Detroit at Cobo Hall.

But on that day, at Lincoln Memorial, after he had delivered a summation of economic and racial injustice, arguing for passage of the Civil Rights Act and extolling the importance of nonviolent protest, Jones says, "One of the world's greatest gospel singers shouted out to one of the world's greatest Baptist preachers." Jones was standing about fifty feet away from King during the speech, when he looked over at Mahalia Jackson, who was standing nearby, and heard her call out to him, "Tell them about the dream, Martin! Tell them about the dream!"[7] Suddenly, it was like a gear in his head turned as he reached deep inside for the language that was ready

---

[6] "I Have a Dream," The Martin Luther King, Jr. Papers, Stanford University. Carson et al. note that King continued to give versions of this speech throughout 1961 and 1962, then calling it "The American Dream." Two months before the March on Washington, King stood before a throng of 150,000 people at Cobo Hall in Detroit to expound upon making "the American Dream a reality."

[7] Emily Crockett, "The Woman Who Inspired Martin Luther King's 'I Have a Dream' Speech," Vox, January 16, 2017.

and waiting. A woman whose ear was keenly attentive to audiences and responses knew the precise note that needed to be struck at that moment. None of the other men shouted this to him. She helped launch him and his dream into history.

Imagination is the ability to face the quotidian challenges of life with an innovative and integrated outlook. Imagination disrupts the familiar, the linear, and the predictable and has a way of demanding attention. George Washington Carver, of the Tuskegee Institute, spoke of "doing common things in an uncommon manner." Or as Einstein is often credited with saying, "Logic will take you from A to B. Imagination will take you anywhere."

According to biblical scholar Walter Brueggemann, imagination is a prophetic calling:

> The prophet does not ask if the vision can be implemented, for questions of implementation are of no consequence until the vision can be imagined. The imagination must come before the implementation. Our culture is competent to implement almost anything and to imagine almost nothing. The same royal consciousness that makes it possible to implement anything and everything is the one that shrinks imagination because imagination is a danger. Thus, every totalitarian regime is frightened of the artist. It is the vocation of the prophet to keep alive the ministry of imagination, to keep on conjuring and proposing futures alternative to the single one the king wants to urge as the only thinkable one.[8]

Thomas E. McCollough, in *The Moral Imagination and Public Life*, defines moral imagination as

> the capacity to empathize with others and to discern creative possibilities for ethical action. The moral imagination

---

[8] Walter Brueggemann, *The Prophetic Imagination*, 2nd ed. (Minneapolis: Augsburg Fortress, 2001), 40.

considers an issue in the light of the whole. The whole is not only the complex interrelated functional aspects of society, economic, political, social institutions. It is also the traditions, beliefs, values, ideals, and hopes of its members, who constitute a community with a stake in the good life and a hopeful future. The moral imagination broadens and deepens the context of decision making to include the less tangible but most meaningful feelings, aspirations, ideals, relationships. It encompasses the core values of personal identity, loyalties, obligations, promises, love, trust, and hope.[9]

McCollough reminds us that "Americans are notoriously pragmatic and prone to be preoccupied with technique, the technological know-how of problem solving."[10] But "values require a broad context of meaning, to which technical reason is oblivious. The pervasive tendency to reduce the scope of reason by limiting knowledge to the technical excludes or ignores humanistic or moral knowledge."[11] What he calls the symbolic imagination allows us to transcend the literal mind, to grasp "the meaning of the whole, including the life of emotions, of unspoken but deeply felt relationships, of aspirations, loyalties and ideals—of what is intended and hoped for, as well as what is done. It involves the whole person, a whole way of life and a vision of life as a whole."[12]

Four days after his arrest in Birmingham on April 12, 1963, Martin Luther King Jr. read a letter in the *New York Times* from several Alabama clergymen criticizing him for stirring up trouble in their city and evoking angry reactions from police and white citizens. As he sat in his jail cell, King penned a reply to the pastors, writing along the margin of the newspaper. It came to be

---

[9] Thomas E. McCollough, *The Moral Imagination and Public Life* (Chatham, NJ: Chatham House Publishers, Inc., 1991), 17.

[10] Ibid.

[11] Ibid., 18.

[12] Ibid.

known as the "Letter from a Birmingham Jail." It is now a classic of moral argument and suasion. But it was a brilliant display of moral imagination to seize the moment to frame a response that was more than a response. We will have more to say of it in the next chapter. Imagination was operating redemptively when the churches of New Orleans gathered for worship after the devastations of Hurricane Katrina in 2005. A United Methodist pastor took a branch from a tree that had fallen and damaged the church building, dipped it into containers of rain water and flung the droplets across the altar upon the gathered survivors who huddled together in gratitude. It was the church's way of declaring that what was meant to destroy us is now making us stronger and freer and wiser.

Cognitive psychologists have studied the processes behind innovation and creativity, and although there is no consensus, many believe there are several elements that we should consider. Scott Barry Kaufman is scientific director of the Imagination Institute at the University of Pennsylvania, a project supported by the Templeton Foundation. He notes that British psychologist Graham Wallas developed a fourfold process that seems effectively to frame creativity.

Wallas suggested that at least four stages are involved: preparation, incubation, illumination, and verification. In the first stage your brain is gathering information. In the second stage you let your mind wander and stretch your ideas. In the third stage, you make connections between ideas. In the fourth stage creative ideas need to be polished by critical thinking in order to persuasively reach their audience.[13]

The research on imagination, creativity, and innovation is interesting, in part, because every act that is intended to depart from the conventional way of doing things constitutes a break with the status quo. This disruption amounts to saying, "No, I will not go

---

[13] See Scott Barry Kaufman, *Wired to Create: Unraveling the Mysteries of the Creative Mind* (New York: Penguin Random House, 2015), 1.

forward according to society's script, I will do a new thing. I will dream up something unique." Such creative departures from the norm, whether the acts of visionaries or of whistleblowers who refuse to tolerate wrongdoing and injustice, should be a part of the conversation about moral leadership in the future.

Centering Down, Stepping Forward, and Dreaming Up to Serve the Common Good

Moral leaders exhibit these qualities in the service of a greater cause, that of serving the *common good*. This is a broad and generous phrase that points to the things we all need and desire for a chance to live a fulfilling life. The founders of the American republic were wise in crafting a shorthand way to express this aspiration. The Preamble to the US Constitution reads:

> We the People of the United States, in Order to form a more perfect Union, establish Justice, insure domestic Tranquility, provide for the common defense, promote the general Welfare, and secure the Blessings of Liberty to ourselves and our Posterity, do ordain and establish this Constitution for the United States of America. (Signed in convention September 17, 1787. Ratified June 21, 1789).[14]

It is hardly necessary to emphasize the obvious discrepancy between this noble rhetoric of inclusion, "We the People" and America's realities of exclusion and oppression, an exclusion that

---

[14] Law professors Erwin Chemerinsky and Michael Stokes Paulsen write that "the Preamble of the U.S. Constitution—the document's famous first fifty-two words—introduces everything that is to follow in the Constitution's seven articles and twenty-seven amendments" (National Constitution Center website, "Interactive Constitution").

was sometimes almost surgical in nature (think of the one drop of Negro blood that makes a person black).[15] Nevertheless, the aspirational horizon of "forming a more perfect Union" continues to inspire many. Even skeptics could be moved hearing Dr. King utter those words after his experience of being arrested, stabbed, spat upon, and hounded by the FBI. Beyond the aspirational power of this vision, an observer like Robert Bellah asserts that "in the crazy quilt of conflicting and overlapping interests, Americans have traditionally, through their legislators and elected officials, been able to discover enough common interest across the discontinuities of region, class, religion, race and sex to order and regulate the affairs of a giant industrial society."[16] Moral leaders like Frederick Douglass, Rosa Parks, Dr. King, and many others have understood, appealed to, and helped unleash "common interest" sufficient to begin dismantling slavery and then segregation.

We should also note that the while the founders were inventing a model of government that placed the common good at the center, they also believed that a great nation required virtuous citizens. Consider this declaration by John Adams, second president of the United States:

> Government is instituted for the common good; for the protection, safety, prosperity and happiness of the people; and not for profit, honor, or private interest of any man, family, or class of men; therefore, the people alone have an incontestable, unalienable, and indefeasible right to institute government; and to reform, alter, or totally change the

---

[15] This practice, known as hypodescent, assigned the child of mixed-race parents to the socioeconomic group of the person (usually woman) of lower status. In 1967, the one-drop rule was invalidated by the US Supreme Court in the famous case of *Loving v. Virginia* predicated on a violation of the equal protection clauses of the Fourteenth Amendment.

[16] Robert N. Bellah, Richard Madsen, William M. Sullivan, Ann Swidler, and Steven M. Tipton, *Habits of the Heart: Individualism and Commitment in American Life* (Berkeley and Los Angeles: University of California Press, 1985), 201.

same, when their protection, safety, prosperity and happiness require it.[17]

Commenting on the Founders' preoccupation with virtue, Thomas G. West suggests that

the founders were far from being concerned only with low bourgeois virtues, such as acquisitiveness, and comfortable self-preservation. In fact, they considered virtue as a condition of freedom and a requirement of the laws of nature. . . . Many public documents from the time spoke of the need for social and republican virtues within the populace such as justice (i.e., obeying the law), moderation, benevolence, temperance, industry, frugality, religious piety, and a responsibility among the people's representatives to secure their good. In times of war, however, virtues of strength such as courage, leadership, bravery, vigor, and manly exertion are required. Virtue is of concern to government not as an end in itself, but as a means to security and ultimately to happiness.[18]

Of course, we know that these same men who spoke eloquently of virtue and republican government were capable of dishonoring treaties with Native Americans, slaughtering them when expedient, and forcing free African people into lifetimes of unpaid labor.

Integrity, Courage, and Imagination for the Common Good, While Inviting Others

Moral leaders exhibit integrity, courage, and imagination as they serve the common good—the good of all the people—while also

---

[17] John Adams, commenting on Article VII of the Constitution of the Commonwealth of Massachusetts, 1780.

[18] Thomas G. West, *The Political Theory of the American Founding: Natural Rights, Public Policy, and the Moral Conditions of Freedom* (Cambridge, UK: Cambridge University Press, 2017).

inviting others to join the movement, the historical process of change. The invitation is an act of humility. No leader can accomplish great purposes alone. The leader acknowledges that others are important and can add value. Invitations can be extended face to face, mediated through various forms of communication, and through social media that provide opportunities to respond immediately and directly to the appeal. I note that, as a nation, America is an invitation to people throughout the world who long for entry to this community of promise. It is hard to imagine a more compelling and generous invitation than the words by Emma Lazarus that are inscribed on the Statue of Liberty (another great colossal monument).

> Give me your tired, your poor,
> Your huddled masses yearning to breathe free,
> The wretched refuse of your teeming shore.
> Send these, the homeless, tempest-tossed to me,
> I lift my lamp beside the golden door![19]

The invitation to join a moral community has always been compromised by tribalism and the determination of a few to control and define precisely who would be welcome in this nation. During the Trump administration we saw how the government itself could deface one of the nation's most treasured monuments by imposing a new hermeneutical or interpretive frame, namely, that the invitation should be understood to include only the tired, huddled masses from Europe who can stand on their own feet. But often the inclusive vision and appealing invitation have emerged in popular culture, best demonstrated in the 1972 number-one hit song, "Love Train" by The O'Jays. The artists are quite explicit about the global reach of the American invitation to refuge, community, and opportunity.

---

[19] Emma Lazarus (1883), "The New Colossus," *Historic American Documents* (1883) (Lit2Go edition).

People all over the world (everybody), Join hands,
Start a love train, love train . . .
Tell all the folks in Russia, and China too,
Don't you know that it's time to get on board . . .
Tell all the folks in Egypt, and Israel, too . . .
Please don't miss this train at the station, Cause
    if you miss it,
I feel sorry for you.[20]

This is a complex definition that addresses virtues and traits of moral leaders, the goal of their action, and their habit of enlisting others. With this working definition in place, we move to consider how moral leaders are identified and how they come to be.

Monuments and Moral Leadership

Public monuments symbolize the values and aspirations of a community. But, monuments are also invitations. The public display of monuments that highlight individuals constitutes an invitation to the viewers to ponder the best of what that community has produced and wishes to instill in current and future generations. When communities reappraise the meaning and value of a monument from the past, they should feel compelled to interpret and contextualize these public choices as expressions of their deeply held memories and values. This is a fascinating process under way in many places and especially volatile across the United States now. Universities and communities are undertaking research to uncover and render transparent their past involvements with human slavery and other tragic practices. Some are choosing to remove names and monuments. Some are adding messages to explain and contextualize them. But many others have not yet

---

[20] The O'Jays, "Love Train," songwriters Kenneth Gamble, Leon Huff, Sony/ATV Music Publishing L.L.C., 1972.

begun this arduous process of moral self-examination and repair.[21]
Writer David Roos observes:

> Public monuments don't emerge out of thin air. They are
> the products of collective human efforts often expensive and
> time-consuming—to honor a person, a group of people or a
> historical event. . . . At some levels, all public monuments are
> statements of power. In ancient Egypt, the pharaohs erected
> pyramids and obelisks as permanent symbols of their immense
> power and eternal influence. In communist regimes colossal
> statues of Lenin, Stalin, Mao and Kim Il Sung are towering
> reminders of the central government's unquestionable author-
> ity. But, you can argue that public monuments dedicated to
> women, civil rights leaders, victims of genocide and martyrs
> to valiant causes are also statements of power. By acknowl-
> edging the achievements and sacrifices of historically less
> powerful groups, *these monuments are ways of taking power from
> their oppressors and (literally) carving their rightful place in history*
> (emphasis added).[22]

We have observed historical markers in Germany that remind
people of the horrific events that unfolded during the Holocaust.
And we have seen monuments to Stalin, Saddam Hussein, and
Confederate leaders like Robert E. Lee pulled down. Universities,
cities, and other communities are reckoning with how to tell their
stories and express their values once they discover and admit that

---

[21] Carly O'Connell of Higher Education Today notes that "the University
of Virginia (UVA) has organized a consortium called Universities Studying
Slavery (USS) that brings together over 40 colleges and universities across
the country and world to share resources as they confront the role of slavery
and racism in their histories and its impact today" ("University Consortium
Addresses History of Slavery and Its Continuing Impact" (October 3, 2018).
See also University of Virginia, President's Commission on Slavery and the
University, "Universities Studying Slavery," online.

[22] Dave Roos, "How Removing Public Monuments Works," HowStuff-
Works/Science.

former donors, leaders, and alumni represented values and goals that contradict the institution's current identity and mission.

The story of the monuments at Mount Rushmore and to Crazy Horse invite reflection on how the present and the past clash and how people can reallocate the power to bestow the goods of honor and recognition.

Consider this hypothetical: The idea for a Mount Rushmore of moral leaders is gaining momentum. You have been invited to serve as an adviser to the concept of a moral Mount Rushmore. Whom would you nominate to be sculpted into the granite? Any four moral leaders—the floor is open. Identify them and justify your choices. Ideally, they should emerge from or represent different sectors, vocations, or life experiences. The nation is diverse, and its symbols of moral excellence should represent some of that diversity.

I teach a class on the principles and practices of moral leadership. Recently I began the course with the moral Mount Rushmore exercise. But years ago I began the course very differently. I used to begin by asking students to define moral leadership by calling out the first words that came to mind on hearing the phrase. They generated a list of virtues and characteristic behaviors expected in moral leaders. This is the list culled from the board on August 31, 2016:

Responsibility	Authenticity	Honest	Perseverance
Accountability	Trustworthy	Forgiving	Transparency
Humility	Visionary	Inspiring	Ambition
Focus	Inclusive	Discerning	Listening
Servant	Hopeful	Self-aware	Contextually aware

Then I stumbled across an article on Mount Rushmore. I had known that the massive outdoor sculpted tribute to four US presidents was built to lure more tourists to the western part of the country. What I did not know was two interesting facts that fascinated me. First, the architect who undertook and supervised the carving at Mount Rushmore was the same artist who was selected to carve the colossal images on Stone Mountain in Georgia. Gutzon Borglum was a brilliant and daring sculptor, but he was also a committed white supremacist. He won wide acclaim for carving the leaders of the Confederacy onto the mountain outside Atlanta, and because of that job, he was selected to do Rushmore.

Second, the four "men on the mountain" are not the original cast. In fact, the selection of the actual number and identity of the figures was quite fluid. Particularly intriguing was the idea that among the preferred or suggested images were Lewis and Clark, Chief Red Cloud, and Buffalo Bill.[23]

Later, serious proposals included Sacagawea, the Lemhi Shoshone Indian explorer who helped Lewis and Clark, and the suffragist Susan B. Anthony.

It is fascinating and exciting to consider that the nation could have had women and people of color alongside these courageous white male presidents as emblems of American identity.[24] Unfortunately, given African American–specific hatred and racism in the United States, no African Americans appear to have ever been considered.

I then showed my students illustrations of persons who might be candidates for this recognition and honor. When students examined this extensive portfolio of possibilities, they became quite animated in discussing the qualities that would qualify or disqualify nominees.

As we debated, we found it important and useful to distinguish people who had engaged in some noteworthy and memorable moral action that expressed their deeply held ethical values and those who seemed to possess a vocation, a calling to live their lives

---

[23] Sam Anderson, "Why Does Mount Rushmore Exist?" *New York Times Magazine* (March 22, 2017).

[24] Rex Alan Smith, *The Carving of Mount Rushmore* (New York: Abbeville Press, 1985); John Taliaferro, *Great White Fathers: The Story of the Obsessive Quest to Create Mount Rushmore* (New York: Public Affairs, 2002).

Mount Rushmore monument

in ways that made them identifiable as moral leaders. Interestingly, notions of consistency, persistence, self-conscious awareness, and self-criticism became more evident and prominent.

We then drew a distinction between people who might be considered moral leaders and those who had exhibited some exquisite but discreet act or episode of moral agency. They did the right things for the right reasons but quickly returned, perhaps retreated, from the expectation of continuing to do so. The call to leadership can be a deep source of fulfillment and adventure. But it can also mean a life in the spotlight, bearing the weight of constant scrutiny and potential conflict or harassment. We can understand why someone might not accept or seek the mantle of moral leadership. And we can still admire people of this kind who possess what author Eyal Press calls "beautiful souls," doing what is right and good when called upon though they do not aspire to life-changing implications of the moral life.

Press writes about several ordinary people who step up in times of moral crisis to do extraordinary things. His book opens with the wonderful words of Susan Sontag, "At the center of our moral life and our moral imagination are the great models of resistance; the great stories of those who have said 'No.'"[25] His examples include a police captain in Switzerland in 1938 "who violates the thing he is duty-bound to enforce—the law—[by rescuing Jewish refugees from Germany] at a time when countries throughout the world were crafting rules that left countless officials like him with a choice between doing their jobs or saving innocents."[26] I like to highlight the whistleblowers in every sector of life who are on the inside of an organization, discover ethical threats, and call attention to them. I was thrilled when the December 2002 issue of *Time* magazine chose to recognize and honor three women whistleblowers on its cover as "Persons of the Year": Cynthia Cooper of WorldCom, Coleen Rowley of the FBI, and Sherron Watkins of Enron. Think of all the good that has come from the courageous agency of people who did not seek to become leaders but made an enormous positive impact on society. I'll mention two of my favorites from the long list of whistleblowers on Wikipedia: Daniel Ellsberg, the military analyst who leaked the Pentagon Papers that revealed "practices of deception by previous administrations and contributed to the erosion of public support for the [Vietnam] war." And Frank Serpico was a former New York City police officer, was the first in the history of the NYPD to expose bribery and other charges before a public commission on police corruption. The list includes many others who have exposed sexism, corruption, racism, and other social evils, thereby setting lasting change in motion.

Changing my approach from discussing lists of virtues to describing virtuous people provided an unexpected pedagogical discovery. Beginning a conversation about moral leadership by asking about disembodied, abstract virtues, traits, and personal character attributes proved to be somewhat sterile and distant. But when

---

[25] Eyal Press, *Beautiful Souls: The Courage and Conscience of Ordinary People in Extraordinary Times* (New York: Farrar, Strauss and Giroux, 2013), 2.

[26] Ibid., 8.

talking about specific people who embodied virtue and were compelling enough to memorialize in stone, the conversation and our brains came alive in a new way.

New York Times journalist and pundit David Brooks makes this point as he explains his biographical method in his book on virtue, *The Road to Character:*

> I will describe what this character-building method looks like in real life. I'm going to do this through biographical essays, which are also moral essays. Since Plutarch, moralists have tried to communicate certain standards by holding up exemplars. You can't build rich . . . lives simply by reading sermons or following abstract rules. Example is the best teacher. Moral improvement occurs most reliably when the heart is warmed, when we come into contact with people we admire and love and we consciously and unconsciously bend our lives to mimic theirs.[27]

It is interesting to compare the history of Mount Rushmore with the current project under way to construct a memorial to Crazy Horse, a symbol of resistance to dominant images of conquest and courage. Certainly he has a claim to be remembered and honored. John Taliaferro writes:

> We have few heroes like Crazy Horse in American history. Unlike Chief Joseph, Crazy Horse never surrendered. Unlike

---

[27] David Brooks, *The Road to Character* (New York: Random House, 2015), xv. He continues, "The subjects of the portraits that follow in chapters 2 through 10 are a diverse set, white and black, male and female, religious and secular, literary and nonliterary. None of them is even close to perfect. But they practiced a mode of living that is less common now. They were acutely aware of their own weaknesses. They waged an internal struggle against their sins and emerged with some measure of self-respect. And when we think of them, it is not primarily what they accomplished that we remember—great though that may have been—it is who they were. I'm hoping their examples will fire this fearful longing we all have to be better, to follow their course" (xvi).

Geronimo, he was never imprisoned. Unlike Red Cloud, he never signed a treaty. Unlike Sitting Bull, he never allowed his shadow to be captured by the camera. He never even slept in a white man's bed. And because his grave is a mystery, for thousands of Indians he is still very much at large. He still lives. Today, numerous places in the Black Hills are named for Custer: a town, a county, a mountain, a state park. But the spirit of Crazy Horse is everywhere. And those who sense his presence also nurture the belief that the Black Hills, like the promised land, may one day belong to the Lakota again.[28]

In comparison to Mount Rushmore, where the heads of four US presidents are 60 feet high, Crazy Horse's head will be 87 feet high and his arm will be 263 feet long. As Borglum was carving Mount Rushmore, some Oglala Lakota elders urged him to add Crazy Horse as the only one worthy to place by the side of Washington and Lincoln, but apparently Borglum never responded.[29] The construction continues, as does the legend of a great warrior who will remind all visitors of the original inhabitants of these sacred lands. Nevertheless, some descendants oppose the effort to honor Crazy Horse in this particular way. One relative noted:

They don't respect our culture because we didn't give permission for someone to carve the sacred Black Hills where our burial grounds are. They were there for us to enjoy and they were there for us to pray. But it wasn't meant to be carved into images, which is very wrong for all of us. The more I

---

[28] John Taliaferro, *Great White Fathers: The Story of the Obsessive Quest to Create Mount Rushmore* (Cambridge, MA: PublicAffairs, Perseus Books Group, 2002), 38–39. Several good biographies of Crazy Horse exist, such as the highly regarded Mari Sandoz, *Crazy Horse: The Strange Man of the Oglalas*, 3rd ed. (Lincoln: University of Nebraska Press, 2008).

[29] Joseph Agonito, *Lakota Portraits: Lives of the Legendary Plains People* (Guilford, CT: TwoDot Book, 2011).

Crazy Horse monument

think about it, the more it's a desecration of our Indian culture. Not just Crazy Horse, but all of us.[30]

This is fascinating and complicated because although the Crazy Horse Memorial appears to represent an act of resistance and pride, of taking back the power to honor, it exposes the determination of some Indians to resist Western habits of recognizing people through physical monuments.

Literature on Leaders, Moral and Otherwise

In ancient societies there was greater curiosity about leadership that was moral, an emphasis that waned as time passed and literate elites seemed to retreat into material and military power and

---

[30] "Crazy Horse Memorial Generates Mixed Feelings," *Voice of America News*, September 13, 2003.

articles in psychology, business, religion, philosophy, anthropology, sociology and political science found only a handful that addressed leadership ethics in any depth. . . .

Given the centrality of ethics to the practice of leadership, it is striking how little systematic research has focused on key questions. How do leaders form, sustain, and transmit moral commitments? Under what conditions are those processes most effective? What is the impact of ethics officers, codes, training programs, and similar initiatives? How do norms and practices vary across context and culture? And, what can we do at the individual, organizational and societal levels to foster moral leadership?[35]

Rhode does acknowledge that the general neglect of moral leadership is rapidly changing. "Moral leadership is now in a boom cycle. At last count, a web search revealed some forty-seven thousand sites. National leaders have clamored that 'Something Must Be Done.'"[36] Rhode's hopeful observation received validation from a couple of leaders who bridge the public-private domains. Michael Bloomberg, a 1966 Harvard Business School MBA graduate and former mayor of New York City, delivered the 2019 Class Day speech at HBS calling on graduates to demonstrate moral leadership. He noted, "Being ethical does not require a master's degree, it requires having a conscience and following it."[37] In a similar spirit, former Secretary of Labor Robert Reich, commenting on the role of presidential leadership, writes:

An American president is not just the chief executive of the United States, and the office he (eventually she) holds is not just a bully pulpit to advance certain policy ideas. He is also

---

[35] Deborah L. Rhode, ed. *Moral Leadership: The Theory and Practice of Power, Judgment, and Policy* (San Francisco: Jossey-Bass, 2006), 3.

[36] Ibid., 1.

[37] Clea Simon, "Bloomberg Extols 'Moral Leadership' at Business School," *Harvard Gazette*, May 30, 2019.

a moral leader, and the office is a moral pulpit invested with meaning about the common good. It is hardly the case that every president has been a moral exemplar, but a president inevitably helps set the moral tone of the nation. The values a president enunciates and demonstrates ricochet through society, strengthening or undermining the common good.[38]

I want to validate the claim that moral leadership is a "greening" field, happily on the increase. Rather than review that literature here, I have added an appendix, describing a number of texts that have especially impressed me.

Few of the valuable texts on moral leadership are written from the unique perspective of persons "behind the veil," as W.E.B. Du Bois would put it. By that, I refer to the underside of history, the outlook of those who join civil society from the margins after centuries of careful observation, skepticism, determination, and hope for a more authentic, inclusive democracy.[39]

I believe that moral leadership is the single most important determinant of a nation's character and the culture of its institutions. Most moral theory assumes the existence of an assimilated, fully formed self, an ego prepared to negotiate with others. My perspective draws front and center the perspectives and experiences of people whom society has sought to relegate to the sidelines, but who nevertheless struggle to rise above discouraging circumstances and lift others as they climb.

Traditional moral theory assumes the absence of historical and ongoing trauma and that individuals simply need a better moral

---

[38] Robert B. Reich, *The Common Good* (New York: Alfred A. Knopf, 2018), 118.

[39] As Emory University scholars Vanessa Siddle Walker and John R. Snarey put it, "No one ethnic-racial group hears the whole truth nor only the truth, but African Americans do acquire a partial superiority of hearing and understanding from the particular place in which they sit at the world's table" (Vanessa Siddle Walker and John R. Snarey, eds., *Race-ing Moral Formation: African American Perspectives on Care and Justice* [New York: Teachers College Press, 2004], 146).

compass to get on with the business of living a moral life. Conventional theorists assume minds can and should reason morally in a deductive manner to arrive at justifiable reasons for doing the right things. In other words, generally speaking, moral theory has been written for middle-class, educated people fully assimilated into the dominant society. Such works have value as they offer wisdom and lessons for a good life. But in a world that has been profoundly affected by hundreds of years of colonization, violence against indigenous populations, theft of land and property, and human enslavement, those worthy perspectives are also problematic. Problematic for the many they fail to engage. A vast portion of the human population has a different starting point in history.

America has always been a divided society, a train traveling on two tracks, not one. Many selves in this country are constructed in the context of oppression and existential threat to their status as a full person. In 1903 W.E.B. Du Bois shed light on this process in *The Souls of Black Folk*: "One ever feels his twoness,—an American, a Negro; two souls, two thoughts, two unreconciled strivings; two warring ideals in one dark body, whose dogged strength alone keeps it from being torn asunder."[40]

It is important to acknowledge that this haunting sense of "twoness" can influence how moral reasoning occurs. Those who feel themselves to be part of a civil society, accepting its legitimacy and values, are likely to reason in ways that support the legitimate social and moral order. But for those who feel they cannot affirm the legitimacy of a social order, civil disobedience is understandable and appropriate. We see this in the decision of Martin Luther King Jr. to break the law and be incarcerated in Birmingham in 1963. After Du Bois, I did not think I would ever find a trope with greater resonance exploring the psychosocial complexity of marginalized moral agents until I discovered words from Cesar Chavez's friend and colleague Luis Valdez.

---

[40] W.E.B. Du Bois, *The Souls of Black Folk* (New York: Penguin, 1903), 1–2.

As a Mexican, I have felt the sting of life among the gringos since the day I was born, some twenty-four years ago in a classic example of the American "small town." . . .

Life sometimes poses difficult questions. Once they are asked, there is no effective way a man can ignore them. He can prod at them like live scorpions. He can suppress them till they turn to acid in his gut. He can drink beer or cheap wine and sing dirty songs or sad *corridos* til he's drunk and he forgets, but they always come back. The shame, the pride, the hate, the love—a fierce mosaic of paradoxical emotions; and always, under them, the same basic questions: "Why do they treat me this way?[41]

One of the books that Dr. King often carried in his briefcase for inspiration and wisdom was *Jesus and the Disinherited* by Howard Thurman, the great theologian, university chaplain, and pastor. In the beginning of that book Thurman writes: "Many and varied are the interpretations dealing with the teachings and life of Jesus of Nazareth. But few of these interpretations deal with what the teaching and the life of Jesus have to say to *those who stand, at a moment in human history, with their backs against the wall.*"

The perspectives of people like Du Bois, Thurman, Dolores Huerta, Ella Baker, and Martin Luther King Jr. inform my thoughts about moral agency and moral leadership. They are especially valuable as I reflect on certain paradigmatic steps that lead from moral indifference, inertia, and ignorance to hope-giving agency and life-transforming leadership. Leadership experts Warren Bennis and Joan Goldsmith refer to them as "crucible experiences," noting that such "difficult and, in some cases, life-threatening events" involve "severe tests of patience or belief, or difficult trials, and they are characterized by a confluence of

---

[41] Quoted in Miriam Pawel, *The Crusades of Cesar Chavez: A Biography* (New York: Bloomsbury Press, 2014), 110.

threatening intellectual, social, economic, or political forces."[42] I will mention two of them here.

First, the call to moral agency and leadership is more often than not accompanied by self-doubt and a sense of inadequacy. The experience of Moses in Exodus, doubting his capacity to serve as God's messenger, illumines this phenomenon. For people behind the veil, there is an added dimension of external societal doubt in the ability of female, minority, or LGBTQ leaders to offer value and vision that the public needs. This is often when the inner resources of a leader are marshaled to enable agency and unleash imagination. The resources of prayer, meditation, song, silence, exhortation, story, and friendship can help those who are living with strain and pain to step forward and press on toward their goals.

Second, there is often the experience of what we might call the midnight terror in Gethsemane—a way of describing an existential encounter with death and nonbeing. There, in the Garden of Gethsemane, Jesus confronted abandonment and loneliness. Dr. King wrote about such an experience after receiving life-threatening phone calls in the middle of the night and how he confronted God amid these core-shaking events. Gethsemane, of course, initiates the long walk to crucifixion at Calvary. Many have had the experience of being falsely accused, targeted, and unjustly tagged with responsibility for some unfortunate outcomes. People who live behind the veil know about Gethsemane, terror, and the cross. And those experiences must be part of the account of the moral life of marginalized people.

When integrity, courage, and imagination take shape under the skeptical gaze of exclusion and oppression, what begins as normative ethics is thrust into metaethics as people ask themselves, "Why

---

[42] Warren Bennis and Joan Goldsmith, *Learning to Lead: A Workbook on Becoming a Leader*, 4th ed. (New York: Basic Books, 2010), 86. The authors also note: "Leaders often find that in these crucibles they forge a new identity when they find in themselves the wherewithal to overcome their crises and come through them transformed into more capable leaders."

should I be moral when the moral systems that evaluate me are profoundly unfair?" Or, as we shall see, young Martin Luther King Jr. asked himself, "How can I love those who hate me?" Authentic moral leaders feel obliged and privileged to adopt the moral high ground, even as the larger society behaves unfairly, realizing that the ultimate force of good and righteousness in the universe will align with those who step forth to do right. In the face of immoral tactics and rhetoric, former first lady Michelle Obama's exhortation, "When they go low, we go high," was a compelling restatement of the necessity of attempting to elevate and transform discourse in the public square.

Fortunately, these crucible experiences are also comprehensible enough to those who are not members of marginal communities. That is the promise and the power of empathy and solidarity. That is the beauty of becoming an ally of someone who may suffocate behind and within the veil. That is why agency and "ally-ship" represent a hopeful connection in a divided world.

So, throughout this little volume, I occasionally allude to insights that are informed by my own identity as a curious and hopeful African American man who has lived long enough—since the US Supreme Court declared segregation unconstitutional in the case of *Brown v. Board of Education* in 1954—to see many positive changes in this nation, while acknowledging there is more to be done, and who is preparing his granddaughters for the world while preparing the world for them.

Becoming a Moral Agent and Leader: Developmental Insights

Whether the figures on Mount Rushmore, modern presidents, or others—whether fairly or not—hold up as moral leaders, it is important to remember that all of them were shaped by communities with values. No thinker highlights the developmental journey more compellingly than the late Harvard psychoanalyst Erik Erikson.

Psychiatrist and author Robert Coles, who worked with Erikson at Harvard, said he was deeply imprinted by "Erikson's attempts to understand the nature of moral leaders—as in his studies of Luther and Gandhi" and that "Erikson's own moral leadership, for many of us trained in psychoanalytic psychiatry, would be decisive."[43] For myself, while at Harvard Divinity School in the 1970s, I found Erikson's work to be helpful for its rich personal and cultural insights and diagnostic sophistication. At the same time, Erikson had his blind spots and things about which he would undoubtedly have learned and grown, particularly about gender and race, if he had lived longer. Nevertheless, he took risks to better understand the lives of unfamiliar moral agents and leaders who were seeking to serve the common good and inviting the world to join him. One example was in his seminars and dialogues with Huey P. Newton, founder of the Black Panther Party, captured in *In Search of Common Ground*.[44]

Erikson's books provide powerful tools for understanding the upheavals and revolutions that unfolded in America during the post–World War II period. They include *Childhood and Society* (1950), *Identity and the Life Cycle* (1959), *Identity, Youth, and Crisis* (1968), and *The Life Cycle Completed: Extended Version* (1997). I summarize here his theory of developmental stages.

Erikson suggests that an individual grows through the human lifecycle engaged in an ongoing process of negotiating biological and sociocultural forces. At each new threshold of development from infancy through childhood to adolescence, young adulthood, mature adulthood, and the elder years, humans must successfully reconcile these conflicting forces and achieve the trait or virtue of each stage. If successful, one enters the new stage with certain assets. If not successfully managed, one may proceed, as one grows older, still working through the challenges of an earlier developmental crisis.

---

[43] Coles, *Lives of Moral Leadership*, 205.

[44] Erik H. Erikson and Huey P. Newton, *In Search of Common Ground* (New York: W. W. Norton and Co., 1974).

Approximate Age	Psychosocial Crisis/Task	Virtue Developed
Infant — 18 months	Trust vs Mistrust	Hope
18 months — 3 years	Autonomy vs Shame/Doubt	Will
3–5 years	Initiative vs Guilt	Purpose
5–13 years	Industry vs Inferiority	Competency
13–21 years	Identity vs Confusion	Fidelity
21–39 years	Intimacy vs Isolation	Love
40–65 years	Generativity vs Stagnation	Care

Erikson's Development Stages

Our purpose is not to suggest that understanding the makeup of moral leaders requires us to psychoanalyze them or ourselves. Rather, Erikson, Robert Coles, and fellow theorists provide important categories and questions. For instance, when a child is being reared in a nurturing, loving home, what benefits does that child derive? And how do those benefits translate into the development of promising traits, emotions, and behaviors that are important for moral leaders?

These questions can be useful for enhancing our appreciation of the qualities that leaders exhibit, but they can also help us highlight leaders' shortcomings and the dangers that may be detected early for their good and the good of everyone else. In other words, developmental psychology and, to some extent neuroscience, can illumine dimensions of human being, nature, and possibility that can serve as valuable diagnostic tools for both leaders and caregivers. Too often, undiagnosed challenges (for instance, a profound identity crisis or inability to trust in a relationship) can stifle a person's chances to live a fulfilled life. From a clinical point of view, I served as a hospital chaplain for many years, and I saw the power of gently and respectfully nudging people who were stuck in a stage or at a threshold and needed a little coaxing, coaching, and push to make it over.

It is fascinating to see how Erik Erikson, a secular humanistic developmental psychologist, employs explicit moral categories and ideas to describe the process of people-making.[45] The virtues that he suggests result from our healthy stage-specific conflict resolution, virtues like care, hope, purpose, and love that, if we allow them some currency, are essential for healthy personhood and for moral agency and leadership.

Scholars like Vanessa Siddle Walker and John R. Snarey have highlighted the "failure to include African American perspectives in theory and research on moral formation" that "leads to a failure to include a voice central to developing a more useful, pluralistic psychology of morality and education."[46] Their book *Race-ing Moral Formation* aims to revise moral development theories, particularly those of Lawrence Kohlberg and Carol Gilligan. They present internal black community practices of caregiving, nurture, and forming perspectives on social justice that have contributed to the resilience and agency of countless young people who might otherwise have been profoundly harmed by hostile and racist school environments.[47]

But I note that there has been scholarly debate about the applicability or universalizability of Western developmental stage theories to non-Western, premodern, or traditional societies. In *Cross Cultural Human Development*, Robert L. Monroe and Ruth H. Monroe study the experience of three societies: the Ainu of Japan, the Trobrianders of Melanesia, and the Gusii of East Africa. They draw comparisons and contrasts that are very interesting. For instance, the "linguistic generalization that children everywhere go through one-word and two-word phases in grammatical development, though still based on very incomplete evidence, appears to represent a true developmental universal—one that has weighty implications for theories of human behavior."[48] But when it comes to the "grand

---

[45] The brilliant work of Don S. Browning and colleagues at the University of Chicago Divinity School have contributed to an illuminating dialogue between theology and the social sciences.

[46] Walker and Snarey, *Race-ing Moral Formation*, 14.

[47] Ibid., 77, 96.

[48] Robert L. Monroe and Ruth H. Monroe, *Cross Cultural Human Development* (New York: Jason Aronson, 1975), 152.

schemes of development" like the higher levels we find in Erikson's stages, they "sound suspiciously like modern man and no other." In the end, however, they acknowledge that "the lower stages of these same theories [that is, Erikson's *basic trust* and Piaget's *sensorimotor intelligence*] point to developmental characteristics that have great cross-cultural promise," and research should be continued.[49]

King in Critical Perspective

In this book I intend to examine at length the life of Martin Luther King Jr. for clues about moral agency and moral leadership. I do that, making allowance for stories that have long been circulated about certain of King's personal failings, particularly his infidelities. We have known that, like many biblical personalities, King was fully human, fully fleshed, and fully flawed. Most Americans have reconciled that knowledge with their estimation of King's towering contributions to American history.

Nevertheless, it raises questions that deserve to be acknowledged. This is especially so in light of the report in 2019 by David Garrow, a Pulitzer Prize–winning biographer of Martin Luther King Jr. on newly discovered FBI files alleging outrageous private behavior by Dr. King. This is said to have included observing a rape by a clergy friend.[50] Garrow felt it was important to release this information now, prior to the FBI tapes that are scheduled to be released in 2027, tapes that may confirm the claims about, or perhaps exonerate, Dr. King.

Others felt differently. Many scholars, as well as civil rights leaders, including King's attorney and adviser, Clarence Jones, urged that the source of these allegations should be treated with deep skepticism. The FBI was anxious to discredit King. How much trust should be accorded to their methods and sources? Many observed that some

---

[49] Ibid.
[50] David Garrow, "The Troubling Legacy of Martin Luther King," *Standpoint*, May 30, 2019.

of the most offensive material is not corroborated beyond a single source who wrote notes in the margins of a surveillance report. We know that the FBI continued to surveil Dr. King, long after it knew he was not a communist threat. Its motive was to embarrass, intimidate, and control him and others. It is alleged, for instance, that the FBI even sent embarrassing audiotapes to his wife, along with letters urging him to avoid humiliation by taking his life.

Nevertheless, the allegations in this new reporting are deeply troubling, and if any of them can be confirmed, they obviously demand condemnation. What do we do with such questions? We may never know why life or the heavens call and use flawed people to do great work. That is a mystery. It is comforting to know that grace abounds, and we can learn from others to be better and do better than they did. Perspective and proportion matter.

I will continue to love King and cherish his impact on a nation and on my life, but I will carry that sharp-edged asterisk in my heart. He was a monumental figure, and some of his flaws may have been monumental—for some people, unforgivable. We should also insist that the government should not violate privacy protected by the Constitution by spying on the private lives of citizens, and information that it uncovers in this vulgar manner does not belong in the public domain.

In the coming years we will reappraise the value and lasting power of King's legacy. What he did for America is unmatched. As the King legacy bends, breaks, and gets remade, we should work to do what he died trying to do—eradicating poverty, violence and racism—all the while remembering Oscar Wilde's insight that "every saint has a past, every sinner has a future."

King in Developmental Perspective

King's life became unusual, even extraordinary, under circumstances that were commonplace, albeit tragic. America had managed to reconcile itself to a profoundly immoral and personally brutal social system that pervaded everyone's life, but seemed to disturb only a vocal few. Many had faced challenges of racial segregation and punishment for disobeying these racist rules. And there were many seeking to dismantle and sabotage a system that was evil, even glaringly evil, after America had just joined in defeating Hitler and Nazi ideologies. Now the focus was on America's willingness to continue as a two-tier, apartheid society, or boldly to experiment with rearranging, maybe revolutionizing, the status quo.

As history records, Martin Luther King Jr.'s emergence as a leading voice of the civil rights movement occurred when he was asked to address a gathering in the Holt Street Church in Montgomery to discuss how to respond to the arrest of Rosa Parks for refusing to yield her seat to a white passenger on a public bus. With less than an hour to prepare, the young minister, only twenty-six, stood before the crowd and delivered a speech that galvanized the audience.

Why did King step forward when the people called him? He was reluctant to volunteer for an assignment that appeared to be without boundaries and all consuming. He had crafted a disciplined life with strong guardrails. He had things to do. He was a relative newlywed. He was a new father, his wife, Coretta, a new mother. They were learning to live together as a couple with a baby. He was the new pastor of the Dexter Avenue Baptist Church. He followed a pastor who had strained the good will of many of his parishioners. He had to prove himself and assure this middle-class, educated church that he would not bring about embarrassment and controversy. He had been chosen, in part, because he was a student of Benjamin Mays, a Morehouse man who would bring dignity, polish, and intellectual stature to the pulpit. His call was, as Martin Marty once put it, to "preach short, intellectual sermons to a silk-stocking congregation" and function as the chaplain to a private club. There was much at stake in King's decisions affecting his public profile. He had to calculate any new invitation carefully.

If he had given a mediocre set of perfunctory remarks on that first night of the rally to begin the bus boycott, things could have gone very differently. People would have concluded that he was very young and promising but still immature, not ready for this particular assignment. There were other ministers and lawyers and community leaders they could choose from. After the early success of that meeting and the first days of the boycott, why did he allow himself to be slowly transformed into the spokesperson, face, voice, and symbol of this burgeoning movement?

Instead he gave an amazing and memorable address that changed the course of his own life and the history of this nation. The fact is, following NAACP leader Rosa Parks's example of courageous leadership, he had to respect and listen to what was percolating around him. He could not ignore this movement and also remain faithful to his deeply held beliefs. In order to follow Jesus of Nazareth, he had to listen and interrupt the flow of his routines.

As I ponder these questions in the life of a moral agent who was now being called to become a moral leader, I find value in developmental theories and the explanatory insights that they provide.

Let's consider a few experiences in King's early life that may shed light on the motivational orientation for all the large vocational questions with which he grappled later. Our purpose is not to undertake a full psycho-biographical study of King, a worthy project but far beyond my aim here. Given the pivotal role that this American had on transforming modern America, we all should show greater appreciation and respect for his leadership and sacrifice.

As I reflect on pivotal events in the childhood and youthful development of Martin Luther King Jr. in light of Erikson's model, I am intrigued by an experience that King wrote about in his autobiography:

> From the very beginning I was an extraordinarily healthy child. It is said that at my birth the doctors pronounced me a one hundred percent perfect child from a physical point of view. . . . I hardly know how an ill moment feels. I guess the same would apply to my mental life.[51]

---

[51] Martin Luther King Jr., *The Autobiography of Martin Luther King, Jr.,* ed. Clayborne Carson (New York: Warner Books, 1998), 3.

Even allowing for a bit of hyperbole, King reflects a robust sense of self-confidence and efficacy. He feels the good fortune, the blessings, of a strong constitution and good health. But soon external reality affected him.

> My mother confronted the age-old problem of the Negro parent in America: how to explain discrimination and segregation to a small child. She taught me that I should feel a sense of "somebodiness" but that on the other hand I had to go out and face a system that stared me in the face every day saying you are "less than," you are "not equal to." She told me about slavery.[52]

He notes with appreciation the gift of his loving parents, a strong sense of personal value and ego strength.

King also highlights the difficult conversations that black families must have with their children about the history, manifestations, depths, certainties, and uncertainties of a society built on racist assumptions of black inferiority. Despite a family's heroic efforts to buffer a young child from the brutalities of the external world, the "age-old problem of the Negro parent" entails inherent complications and limits to what parents can achieve. At some point the children must learn and internalize the rules of engagement. The rules must become their rules and be woven into the fabric of the self so that their behavior flows confidently and cautiously from this deep awareness and knowing. The more emotionally charged challenge comes with negotiating highly ambiguous situations where the rules may not be applied in a straightforward way. This resembles high-level casuistry and moral discernment that young children should not have to face. Typically, this conversation—the "talk"—is fraught with dread, regret, anger, and frustration but also with life-preserving urgency. If parents do not transmit this information, harm or death may be the result for the unsuspecting child.

---

[52] Ibid.

I was about six years of age. From the age of three I had a white playmate who was about my age. We always felt free to play our childhood games together. He did not live in our community, but he was usually around every day; his father owned a store across the street from our home. At the age of six we both entered school—separate schools, of course. I remember how our friendship began to break as soon as we entered school; this was not my desire but his. The climax came when he told me one day that his father had demanded that he would play with me no more. I never will forget what a great shock this was to me. I immediately asked my parents about the motive behind such a statement.

We were at the dinner table when the situation was discussed, and here for the first time I was made aware of the existence of a race problem. I had never been conscious of it before. As my parents discussed some of the tragedies that had resulted from this problem and some of the insults they themselves had confronted on account of it, I was greatly shocked, and from that moment on I was determined to hate every white person. As I grew older and older this feeling continued to grow.

My parents would always tell me that I should not hate the white man, but that it was my duty as a Christian to love him. The question arose in my mind: How could I love a race of people who hated me and who had been responsible for breaking me up with one of my best childhood friends? This was a great question in my mind for a number of years.[53]

How deeply was King wounded by these affronts and the reckoning with the newly conceptualized issue of racial discrimination as a child? We cannot know for certain, but he clearly wanted readers to appreciate the pain and self-doubt that are inflicted on children of color by arbitrary personal and systemic assaults. King

---

[53] Ibid., 7.

was nurtured in a loving and safe household and developed a healthy sense of trust. As he observed in an autobiographical essay, "It is quite easy for me to think of a God of love mainly because I grew up in a family where love was central and where lovely relationships were ever present." Then, more pertinently, he continues: "It is quite easy for me to think of the universe as basically friendly, mainly because of my uplifting hereditary and environmental circumstances. It is quite easy for me to lean more toward optimism than pessimism about human nature mainly because of my childhood experiences."[54] King had the psychosocial health that is desired and expected for young children, although the external situation he faced was brutal.

King wrote much about his family and its nurturing ecology. There were three children in the family, and he was the middle child. He was especially conscious of his status relative to his older sister. She seemed to be a confident agent who was the pioneer, charting new childhood paths and experiences. He writes:

> I joined the church at the age of five. I well remember how this event occurred. Our church was in the midst of the spring revival, and a guest evangelist had come down from Virginia. On Sunday morning the evangelist came into our Sunday school to talk to us about salvation, and after a short talk on this point he extended an invitation to any of us who wanted to join the church. My sister was the first one to join the church that morning, and after seeing her join I decided that I would not let her get ahead of me, so I was the next. I had never given this matter a thought, and even at the time of my baptism I was unaware of what was taking place. From this it seems quite clear that I joined the church not out of any dynamic conviction, but out of a childhood desire to keep up with my sister.[55]

---

[54] Carson, *The Autobiography*, 2.
[55] Ibid., 6.

The psychosocial dynamics here are complex. First, King is both an autonomous and self-confident middle child but also anxious about being less highly achieved and esteemed than his sister. I have known Dr. Christine King Farris for over thirty years, and our many chats about her family and Martin suggest that he was complicated and, to her, amusing in that respect. She once reported that he had a group of friends who looked to him as their leader and he maintained that posture until he discovered that his sister was doing some new, cool thing of which he was not yet a part. "Then he would be sweet to me, and I would help him or tell him about some opportunity, then he would go back and make the friends think it was his idea. Yes, that was Martin."[56]

Another of his childhood reflections sheds light on how he observed and learned to manage his anger over injustice and harm to people whom he loved:

> I always had a resentment towards the system of segregation and felt that it was a grave injustice. I remember a trip to a downtown shoe store with Father when I was still small. We had sat down in the first empty seats at the front of the store. A young white clerk came up and murmured politely:
>
> "I'll be happy to wait on you if you'll just move to those seats in the rear."
>
> Dad immediately retorted, "There's nothing wrong with these seats. We're quite comfortable here."
>
> "Sorry," said the clerk, "but you'll have to move."
>
> "We'll either buy shoes sitting here," my father retorted, "or we won't buy shoes at all."
>
> Whereupon he took me by the hand and walked out of the store. This was the first time I had seen Dad so furious. That experience revealed to me at a very early age that my

---

[56] Conversation with Dr. Christine King Farris after worship service, Ebenezer Baptist Church, Atlanta, January 1998.

father had not adjusted to the system, and he played a great part in shaping my conscience.[57]

It is fascinating to note here that King himself was part of a micro-drama that involved refusing to change his seat in a segregated establishment after occupying a comfortable one. One wonders if this memory danced in his head as he learned of Rosa Parks's civil disobedience in December 1955. King already knew that he could triumph if he maintained the emotional, intellectual, and moral high ground. He would provide a framework for understanding this evil system and would unleash the power of his mind and voice to frame and narrate a drama that ordinary people would enact with divine partnership.

Then there was the occasion when the elder King with his son were stopped by the police. Daddy King accidentally drove past a stop sign, and they were pulled over by the police. The officer said:

"All right, boy, pull over and let me see your license."

My father instantly retorted: "Let me make it clear to you that you aren't talking to a boy. If you persist in referring to me as boy, I will be forced to act as if I don't hear a word you are saying."

The policeman was so shocked in hearing a Negro talk to him so forthrightly that he didn't quite know how to respond. He nervously wrote the ticket and left the scene as quickly as possible.[58]

As a young boy, Martin observed the dignity and the defiance of his father, who walked away from capitalist establishments who wanted his money but tried to humiliate him into compliance. This quality of defiance with dignity would mark King's adult leadership as he faced innumerable challenges later in life. With the many

---

[57] King, *The Autobiography*, 7–8.
[58] Ibid., 8.

police-community conflicts that were prominent during the first two decades of the twenty-first century, one wonders what Daddy King's example might say to young people of color today. Defiance with dignity, politeness wedded to the unmistakable assertion of personhood, equality, and real power.

I think that King's reflections on his passage from the preschool and elementary school years affirm what sociologist Robert B. Hill called "the strengths of black families."[59] These families provided the safe place from the storms of a racist and rejecting society. Those struggles continued into King's adolescence, and his reflections grew more insightful and penetrating even as the wounds reached deeper and his inner strength and resourcefulness welled up to meet them.

Once King upset the equilibrium of his Sunday school class by denying doctrine. We can imagine how this was heard and processed by the teacher who heard the pastor's son openly declare heresy. King writes:

I guess I accepted biblical studies uncritically until I was about twelve years old. But this uncritical attitude could not last long, for it was contrary to the very nature of my being. I had always been the questioning and precocious type. At the age of thirteen, I shocked my Sunday School class by denying the bodily resurrection of Jesus. Doubts began to spring forth unrelentingly.[60]

If his class was shocked, it is likely that King's own intellectual development had advanced to a critical and probing stage that his peers did not yet experience or admit to publicly. Once again, he

---

[59] Robert B. Hill, *The Strengths of Black Families* (Lanham, MD: University Press of America, 2003). This book was first published in 1972, when Hill was director of research for the National Urban League, then led by Vernon E. Jordan.

[60] King, *The Autobiography,* 6.

was a lone courageous soul, leading—leading thought and the possibility of a more adequate faith.

In the earlier encounters related above, King was being mentored by his father. But, as he grew into his teenaged years, he would have to negotiate these public racial dramas on his own. He referred to one of those occasions as "the angriest I have ever been":

> There was a pretty strict system of segregation in Atlanta. . . . I went to high school on the other side of town—to Booker T. Washington High School. I had to get the bus in what was known as the Fourth Ward and ride over to the West Side. In those days, rigid patterns of segregation existed on the buses, so that Negroes had to sit in the backs of buses. . . .
>
> When I was fourteen, I traveled from Atlanta to Dublin, Georgia, with a dear teacher of mine, Mrs. Bradley. I participated in an oratorical contest there and I succeeded in winning the contest. My subject, ironically enough, was "The Negro and the Constitution." . . .
>
> That night, Mrs. Bradley and I were on a bus returning to Atlanta. Along the way, some white passengers boarded the bus, and the white bus driver ordered us to get up and give the whites our seats. We didn't move quickly enough to suit him, so he began cursing us. I intended to stay right in that seat, but Mrs. Bradley urged me up, saying we had to obey the law. We stood in the aisle for ninety miles to Atlanta. That night will never leave my memory. It was the angriest I have ever been in my life. . . .
>
> All of these things did something to my growing personality.[61]

Again we see King's negative encounter with segregated busses as a memorable and deeply troubling aspect of his journey from childhood to adulthood.

---

[61] Ibid., 8–9.

The developmental framework of Erikson provides us with one model for helping us to think more systematically about the larger social ecology in which we all grow from childhood to maturity. It also enables us to observe more thoughtfully the development of others, particularly leaders. Ultimately, the goal is to appreciate and understand the various seasons of growth and rites of passage through which humans live and to support the healthiest possible path for that development. In many cases this seemingly personal lifecycle model can offer clues about what parental, familial, community, and social structural actions are necessary for a good passage. And some people believe that stage theory also offers a way to predict where leaders should be headed in their emotional, cognitive, and moral development.

Moral agency and leadership often begin with the desire stirred by curiosity and observation. It is a form of love that draws another person in. It is not love at first sight, but love through repeated sight, observation, and study. Integrity, courage, and imagination develop through knowledge, desire, and practice. Habits form and the wet cement of character is poured into that form or mold. Character develops and hardens.

Helen Vendler says that it is the privilege and responsibility of teachers to teach their students to love what they have loved. I saw this happen up close in two places that I write about, Morehouse College and the Chautauqua Institution. In a later chapter I say more about both, and about how moral leaders may be products of enduring institutions with strong cultures. Before that, however, we consider how moral leaders think and behave.

2

What Moral Leaders Think and Do

Ever tried. Ever failed. No matter. Try again.
Fail again. Fail better.

—SAMUEL BECKETT

If you do not answer the noise and urgency
of your gifts, they will turn on you. Or drag
you down with their immense sadness at be-
ing abandoned.

—JOY HARJO

At Morehouse College, one of America's small liberal arts colleges known for leadership development, when the president stands before a full auditorium of students, there is a special magic in the air. Here, more than any other small school in the nation, there is a shared sense of possibility and what legendary former president Benjamin E. Mays called "an air of expectancy." For here are seated nearly two thousand young men who have negotiated the challenges, barriers, stereotypes, discouragements, disappointments, doubts, insults, and occasional assaults of many in their communities and in the larger society who hindered or doubted their progress. But here also are the hopes, prayers, aspirations, dreams and fulfill-ments of a multitude of families, sacrificing mothers, proud fathers, jubilant siblings, supportive congregations, determined elementary and high school teachers and staffs, and resilient villages that have sent some of their best and brightest for further enlightenment and refinement.

This is my favorite photograph, a portrait of the dreamer as a very young man. He had arrived at a place with a strong culture of care and discipline that would assist his cognitive and character development. And in this community, seated alongside other learners, he would begin to forge the inner resolve to integrate his thought and action.

Martin Luther King Jr., third from left, front row, at Morehouse College

Although very young for college life, King was now in an environment that could empower him for agency and leadership. That process began by allowing and encouraging intellectual honesty about his evolving beliefs, something he longed for. Morehouse encouraged students to experiment with methods for disabling and dismantling segregation. King writes:

> At the age of fifteen, I entered Morehouse College. . . . My days in college were very exciting ones. There was a free

atmosphere at Morehouse, and it was there I had my first frank discussion on race. The professors . . . encouraged us in a positive quest for a solution to racial ills. I realized that nobody there was afraid. Important people came in to discuss the race problem rationally with us.[1]

King's comment about "important people" speaking to the student body makes me smile. I recall sitting in Sale Hall in the middle of the old campus as leaders from around the world addressed us. Of all the speakers during those years, I remember especially the stories told by theologian Howard Thurman, who spoke to us about finding and allowing inner peace to radiate outward to affect others; and by New York Assemblyman Arthur Eve, who reported on the violent resolution of the prisoner revolt at Attica Prison. As Eve spoke of trying to effect a peaceful resolution that resulted in the tragic shooting of several Attica prisoners, tears came to his eyes, and by the end of that chapel assembly there was not a dry eye in the hall.

In this chapter I propose that moral leaders think and act in particular ways that distinguish them from others. *A moral leader is a lifelong student of the moral life and the just society.* These two ancient topics are intellectual preoccupations for moral leaders. The most prominent themes that guide their work will vary from person to person, but fundamentally they are or should be thinking about what makes for a personal life of meaning, purpose, goodness, and righteousness. They think about and work to cultivate communities that enable human flourishing—personal and social transformation.

Although King is useful to illustrate the phenomenon of being a student of the moral life, it is valuable to consider others whose paths and vocation were different. In this regard I also highlight

---

[1] Martin Luther King Jr., *The Autobiography of Martin Luther King, Jr.,* ed. Clayborne Carson (New York: Warner Books, 1998), 13.

elements of the lives of three other people who made an impact on American history: the civil rights activist and King's colleague Ella Baker, and farmworker activists Cesar Chavez and Dolores Huerta.

As we look at Dr. King (1929–68), we find that he focused on the themes of love, power, and justice (all of which were manifest in nonviolence) following three of his post-college intellectual influences, Gandhi, Paul Tillich and Reinhold Niebuhr. I elaborate on his journey through these intellectual sources because these themes will certainly be part of, if not central to, any adequate ethical system that comprises the moral compass of the moral leader.

Ella Baker (1903–86) was born in Norfolk, Virginia, and active in the National Association for the Advancement of Colored People (NAACP). She was among the founders of the Southern Christian Leadership Conference (SCLC) that elected King as its first president in 1957. She ran the Atlanta office of the SCLC and was known for clashing with King and the other male leaders "who allegedly were not used to receiving pushback from strong-willed women. Three years later, she played a key role in supporting students who launched the Student Nonviolent Coordinating Committee, and then left SCLC. Her legacy has been documented in the 1981 documentary film *Fundi: The Story of Ella Baker*. Fundi, her nickname, was "from a Swahili word that means a person who passes down a craft to the next generation."[2] This theme reinforces the point about moral leaders who are generative (using Erikson's term) and who build enduring institutions for the next generation.

Dolores Huerta (1930–), along with Cesar Chavez (1927–93), founded the National Farmworkers Association, which later became the United Farm Workers (UFW). Although both have become icons of the movement for farmworkers' rights, Chavez is much

---

[2] Editors, "Ella Baker Biography," Biography.com, February 28, 2018.

better known, with state holidays in Texas and California. Biographers note that Huerta warrants greater attention as she was the most important Chicana and Latina icon of the twentieth century and continued long into the twenty-first century through her leadership of the Dolores Huerta Foundation established in 2003.[3]

In 1955, the same year that Rosa Parks engaged in civil disobedience to protest Jim Crow segregation law and custom, Dolores Huerta founded the Community Service Organization's branch in Stockton, California. Developing almost in parallel with the southern civil rights movement, Chicanx and Latinx leaders discovered the power of strikes, boycotts, and nonviolent mass action. Two powerful portraits of activism were emerging in the South and the West. Similar to the complementary leadership roles of Ella Baker and Martin Luther King Jr. in the South was the relationship of Cesar Chavez and Dolores Huerta.

> Chavez was the visible leader and Huerta was the "hidden" one. He functioned as the catalyst; she was the engine. Most people did not realize the qualities Huerta brought to the Farm Workers Association: personal strength, communication skills, an ethic of work, intellectual approach, and a strong sense of self. . . . Farm workers listened to her; young Chicanas followed her. . . . To understand Chavez and the union, we must also understand Huerta.[4]

In 2015, the city of Napa unveiled two 9 foot tall statues honoring the pioneering farm worker rights activists and affirming the large Latinx population of Napa Valley, many of whom have helped generate the revenues for the wine and tourist industries there.

---

[3] Stacey K. Sowards, *Sí, Ella Puede!: The Rhetorical Legacy of Dolores Huerta and the United Farm Workers* (Austin: University of Texas Press, 2019).

[4] Richard Griswold del Castillo and Richard A. Garcia, *Cesar Chavez: A Triumph of Spirit* (Norman: University of Oklahoma Press, 1995), 59.

Moral Leaders Are Students
of the Moral Life and Just Society

Moral leaders should have intellectual curiosity and clarity about the moral life and the good community, about individual and social transformation. Although conceptions of a good life and a good society will vary, any intellectual system must grapple with the problems associated with power, with balancing conflicting interests in a just manner, and with the roles of love, forgiveness, reconciliation, reparation, and healing in a good society. We examine how moral leaders may think about these core ethical issues utilizing the life of Martin Luther King Jr. I do want to emphasize that although all moral leaders must think about the meaning, application, and problems of key concepts like justice, virtue, the good and the right, most people will not and need not become formal students of these topics. I give more attention here to King's wrestling with key ideas like love, power, and justice in order to illustrate one approach to wrestling with and arranging the big ideas that should constitute the "furniture" in the mind of the moral leader.

King is best known for his commitment to leading change for racial justice through nonviolent means, so we start there. King was introduced to nonviolence at a time when he was searching for theological and philosophical coherence and alignment between belief and action.

When I went to Morehouse as a freshman in 1944, my concern for racial and economic justice was already substantial. During my student days I read Henry David Thoreau's essay "On Civil Disobedience" for the first time. Here in this courageous New Englander's refusal to pay his taxes and his choice of jail rather than support a war that would spread slavery's territory into Mexico, I made my first contact with the theory of nonviolent resistance. Fascinated by the idea of refusing to cooperate with an evil system, I was so deeply moved that I reread the work several times.[5]

King had begun to discover and carefully study resources that could help him conceptualize and lyricize the moral obligation of civil disobedience. But he made another important and surprising discovery at Morehouse.

As soon as I entered college, I started working with the organizations that were trying to make racial justice a reality. The wholesome relations we had in the Intercollegiate Council convinced me that we had many white persons as allies, particularly among the younger generation. I had been ready to resent the whole white race, but as I got to see more of white people, my resentment was softened, and a spirit of cooperation took its place. I was at the point where I was deeply interested in political matters and social ills. I could envision myself playing a part in breaking down the legal barriers to Negro rights.[6]

During these important years King made several key discoveries that would influence his future, namely, that nonviolence could be a form of power in the hands of the oppressed, that many whites would step forward as allies in the struggle for equal justice and dismantling segregation, and that institutions like Morehouse could help to nurture the moral leaders that would carry the movement forward.

According to his close aids Wyatt Tee Walker and Andrew Young, with whom I have spoken over the years, King sometimes carried a copy of a little book titled *Love, Power, and Justice* in his monogrammed leather briefcase. While the bible and Howard Thurman's *Jesus and the Disinherited* were always there, the third and fourth items changed, often alternating among works by Reinhold

---

[5] King, *The Autobiography*, 14.
[6] Ibid.

Niebuhr, Benjamin Mays, and Paul Tillich. It is also quite interesting to note that near the end of his life, King sent his lawyer to find Rev. Vernon Johns, the pastor who preceded him at Dexter Avenue Baptist Church.[7] Although Johns was considered by many to be a challenging personality, he was a brilliant preacher who read Hebrew, Greek and Latin. King would have carried Vernon Johns with him for intellectual stimulation, theological depth, and inspiration.

King grappled with these three concepts long before he encountered the literature of Western philosophy and theology and extensive debates about Greek understandings of love: eros, philia, and agape. He was the son of a prominent Christian pastor, living in a household with parents who inculcated values and practices for his survival as a black boy in the South, but also for the young Christian gentleman they hoped he would become. King was steeped in the respectability culture of the black bourgeoisie, of which the Howard University sociologist E. Franklin Frazier scathingly wrote: "Because of its struggle to gain acceptance by whites, the black bourgeoisie has failed to play the role of a responsible elite in the Negro community."[8] Although this was not the case for King's father and grandfather, who used their elite status to resist racism and demand equal treatment before the law while organizing wealth-building strategies.

Love was a promise and a problem. King struggled with the theological claim that faithful Christians are to love others, including their enemies. He noted that whites and others also worshiped in Christian spaces but, as he saw it, something was at work to distort their understanding of the Christian love ethic when it came to race relations. He surmised that their possession of liberty, privilege and power corrupted their ethics. How could such pure motivation

---

[7] Ralph Luker, *The Man Who Invented Freedom: The Papers of Vernon Johns* (Tuscaloosa: University of Alabama Press, forthcoming 2020).

[8] E. Franklin Frazier, *Black Bourgeoisie* (New York: Free Press, 1997), 236.

like love be negated by the presence of power and privilege? And, when two or more powerful people, groups, or entities clashed, neither willing to yield, how could justice and reconciliation ever be achieved? King's quest for intellectual coherence in his theology, faith, and his practice are evident here.

As we walk alongside King as he poses critical questions about the meaning of love, it is important to understand that moral agents wrestle with the process of interpreting concepts and texts that they regard to be authoritative. Whether the text is sacred, like the Bible or Qur'an, or nonreligious, like the US Constitution, texts that have power must be read and interpreted with care, appreciation, and respectful criticism. Criticism is particularly important because many texts contain language that had meaning in an earlier time or place but is not helpful and life-giving in another time and location. A critical reading helps the reader appreciate how to discern and extract the essential moral message and meaning of a text. All moral agents come to a point where they ask questions: What does this mean? What does this say to me? How should I respond to this claim or message?

My point is that the encounter with love, power, and justice was not simply an intellectual exercise for King. The issues and questions arose from his existential situation. Following the important revisionist work on the civil rights movement by the theologian James H. Cone, a proper understanding of a theological concept should begin with its actual situation in life, not its abstract, nonhistorical formal meaning. Cone insists that we always should interrogate our texts. Who wrote this book, this article, this brief, this paper? What were/are their investments and interests in the political-economic-cultural status quo? Are they ultimately seeking to legitimize or to deconstruct injustice, inequality, and past wrongdoing?

King's focus was on the interrelation of love, power, and justice and how it was rooted in his emotionally wrenching and deeply personal and group experience of American discrepancies between democratic rhetoric and Jim Crow reality. Many other excellent studies investigate these dimensions of King's life and thought.[9] Noting the discrepancies of a self-described Christian nation I am appreciative of Franciscan theologian Richard Rohr's words:

> Unfortunately, Christianity has not always had a positive impact on Western civilization and the peoples it has colonized or evangelized. So-called Christian nations are often the most militaristic, greedy, and untrue to the teacher we claim to follow. Our societies are more often based *not* upon the servant leadership that Jesus modeled, but on the common domination and control model that produces racism, classism, sexism, power seeking, and income inequality.[10]

Howard Thurman, Benjamin Mays, George Kelsey, and many other theologians labored to make sense of Christian faith in a virulently racist and Christian civilization.[11] King drew from their wisdom.

This was years before he came upon the work and person of Paul Tillich. Tillich was a successful German theologian until he got on the wrong side of Adolph Hitler. In 1933, he was dismissed from his teaching position at the University of Frankfurt. Coincidentally, Reinhold Niebuhr, one of America's most influential theologians, was visiting Germany that same summer and was impressed with Tillich and invited him to join him at Union Theological Seminary. Tillich taught there from 1933 to 1955. Thereafter he spent seven years at Harvard and four years at Chicago. (These last two

---

[9] Authors include James H. Cone, Clayborne Carson, Lewis Baldwin, Obery Hendricks, Michael Eric Dyson, John Ansbro, Vicki Crawford, Taylor Branch, and David Garrow.

[10] Richard Rohr, Daily Meditation, "Following Jesus," Sunday, January 20, 2019.

[11] Benjamin E. Mays, *The Negro's God: As Reflected in His Literature*, reprint ed. (New York: Wipf and Stock Publishers, 2010); George D. Kelsey, *Racism and the Christian Understanding of Man* (New York: Scribner, 1965).

institutions were my alma maters, and I lived in the glow of admiration and ambivalence people had who knew him.) His most influential book was the 1952 masterpiece, *The Courage to Be*, but the one that captivated King most was the 1954 collection of lectures entitled *Love, Power, and Justice*.[12]

Reconciling Protestant Christian thought and existential philosophy, Tillich writes in 1957: "Doubt is not the opposite of faith; it is one element of faith."[13] That quotation alone might help us better appreciate why King would later choose to write a dissertation about Paul Tillich and Henry Nelson Wieman comparing their conceptions of God. King and Tillich did share some correspondence but they never met, although Tillich expressed a desire to meet this young black American whom he had influenced. In response to Tillich's death in October 1965, King commented, "He helped us to speak of God's action in history in terms which adequately expressed both the faith and the intellect of modern humans."[14]

King's doubts intensified at Morehouse and reached crisis proportions in seminary. Here one thinks about Erikson's idea that adolescence and young adulthood are times for working out one's identity and sense of larger purpose. At Crozer Theological Seminary, then in Chester, Pennsylvania, he read Friedrich Nietzsche's *The Birth of Tragedy, On the Genealogy of Morals,* and *The Will to Power*.[15] King biographer John Ansbro notes that King was disturbed by Nietzsche's attack on Hebrew-Christian ethics as a "glorification of weakness." Nietzsche, according to Ansbro,

---

[12] Paul Tillich, *Love, Power, and Justice* (Oxford: Oxford University Press, 1954).

[13] Paul Tillich, *Systematic Theology*, vol. 2: *Existence and The Christ* (Chicago: University of Chicago Press, 1975), 116.

[14] Statement on death of Tillich, October 1965, The King Center.

[15] Fredrich Nietszche, *The Birth of Tragedy [1872] and The Genealogy of Morals* [1887] (New York: Anchor Books, 1956); *The Will to Power* (New York: Random House, 1968).

argued that we may define goodness as everything that heightens the feeling of power in man, the will to power, power itself, and that we may define as bad whatever is born of weakness. Nietzsche considered happiness to be the feeling that power is growing and that resistance is being overcome. He contended that Christianity with its active pity for all the failures and all the weak was more harmful than any vice since it had made an ideal of anything that contradicts the instinct of the strong for self-preservation. Pity deprives us of the strength that is the essence of life. . . . In *The Genealogy of Morals* Nietzsche charged that Jews and Christians, driven by hatred and resentment against the noble and the powerful, had developed a "slave ethic," which extolled love and compassion for the poor, the powerless, the suffering, the sick, and the ugly as a substitute for the "noble morality" of the ancients, which had promoted the robust ideals of power, self-affirmation, health, and beauty. In *The Will to Power* he attacked the Christian duty to love all humanity as a glorification of weakness. He saw this love as favoring all the suffering, botched, and degenerate, and as fostering the instincts of decadence by denying values such as pride, pathos of distance, great responsibility, exuberant spirits, splendid animality, the instincts that rejoice in war and conquest, the deification of passion, anger, revenge, cunning, adventure, and knowledge.[16]

The Greeks through their drama and Olympic games showed us noble examples of human fulfillment, and the Romans, through their empire with paved roads and a vast military, projected control, order, and the beauty of power to the ends of the known world.

---

[16] John J. Ansbro, *Martin Luther King, Jr.: Nonviolent Strategies and Tactics for Social Change* (Charles Scribner's Sons, 1950, renewed 1977 by Paul Ramsey), 2. For a study of King's personal experiences and thinking in seminary, see Patrick Parr, *The Seminarian: Martin Luther King Jr. Comes of Age* (Chicago: Lawrence Hill Books, 2018).

Why shouldn't those values inspire and order our aspirations? It is chilling to see how this outlook has come to pervade much of the political and ideological landscape of contemporary America. Instead, Jesus and the Christianity that followed extolled the virtues of modesty, reverence, resignation, moderation, piety, pity, leniency, simplicity, and obedience. Nietzsche's contempt for the oppressed, the discontented, the diseased, and the mediocre was sharp edged. And King, the seminarian, "had about concluded that Jesus' ethical message of 'Turn the other cheek' and 'Love your enemies' is effective only in conflicts among individuals, not in resolving conflicts among groups, and nations."[17]

In the midst of this crisis, "one Sunday afternoon [King] traveled to Philadelphia to hear a sermon" on Mahatma Gandhi's life and philosophy delivered by Dr. Mordecai Wyatt Johnson, who had just returned from India.[18] Johnson went on to become the first black president of Howard University. King did what any good student does after hearing a sermon or lecture that electrifies the imagination. He read several books on Gandhi. Ansbro reports that "this reading soon restored his original faith in the power of love. He recognized that when love pervades nonviolent methods, far from being a symptom of weakness, it is a potent force for social transformation.[19] Love could be a social force.

Years later, in describing the Montgomery Bus Boycott, the revolution that Rosa Parks and the women of Montgomery drove forward, he explained that Christ had furnished the spirit and the motivation, while Gandhi had provided the method. Although King had read Plato, theologians like Anders Nygren, ethicists like Paul Ramsey on eros, philia and agape: "Gandhi was probably the first person in history to lift the love ethic of Jesus above mere interac-

---

[17] Ansbro, *Martin Luther King, Jr.: Nonviolent Strategies and Tactics for Social Change*, 2.

[18] King, *The Autobiography*, 24.

[19] Ansbro, *Martin Luther King, Jr.: Nonviolent Strategies and Tactics for Social Change*, 3.

tion between individuals to a powerful and effective social force on a large scale."[20]

Gandhi was assassinated in 1948, the same year King graduated from Morehouse and was ordained a Baptist minister. Gandhi was long gone by the time of King's leadership of the Montgomery Bus Boycott in 1955. By 1959, King was finally able to make his own pilgrimage to India and spent a month traveling throughout the subcontinent, meeting the disciples of Gandhi, who were now running the newly independent nation.[21]

The important point is that King emerged from seminary with a renewed sense of love as a soul force that could be a social force. King writes:

> It was in this Gandhian emphasis on love and nonviolence that I discovered the method for social reform that I had been seeking. The intellectual and moral satisfaction that I failed to gain from the utilitarianism of Bentham and Mill, the revolutionary methods of Marx and Lenin, the social contracts theory of Hobbes, the "back to nature" optimism of Rousseau, the superman philosophy of Nietzsche, I found in the nonviolent resistance philosophy of Gandhi.[22]

Coherence was dawning. King, a Christian, had found in a Hindu, Gandhi, a new way to think about how to resist and to reject the inner violence of the spirit. Even this intellectual move

---

[20] King, *The Autobiography*, 24.

[21] King's international travels compose a fascinating story themselves, beginning with his 1957 trip to Ghana to witness the inauguration of Kwame Nkrumah as president of a newly independent nation, two years after the historic Bandung Conference in Indonesia where leaders of independence movements from Africa, Asia, and the developing world gathered. Malcolm X and author Richard Wright attended, and Wright described the consequential meeting in his book *The Color Curtain: A Report on the Bandung Conference*. King's trip to India followed all of this.

[22] King, *The Autobiography*, 24.

was risky in a conservative Christian culture. Few people who sat in those black churches or marched on the streets listening to Martin preach knew that he was fusing Hindu and Eastern thought into his social-gospel Christianity, but King regarded this as a deeper understanding of truth. Indeed, truth could not be contained in a single religious tradition. Truth is a force that manifests itself everywhere. That is why one needs to examine concepts like truth, nonviolence, love, power, and justice comparatively, but also from a deeper, perhaps the deepest conceivable, perspective. Far deeper than sociology (his college major), social science, natural science, or comparative religion, King discovered that he needed that branch of philosophy—which itself etymologically is the love or friend of wisdom; philia (friend) and Sophia (wisdom)—known as ontology, the study of being, the nature of existence.

This is another important dimension of the evolution of the moral leader as a student of the moral life; as one continues to proceed along the lifecycle, the key resources and dialogue partners may also evolve. King had now moved from Sunday School lessons that emphasized the obligation to love others, to his high school and college skepticism that brought him to Henry David Thoreau and civil disobedience, and on to seminary, where he encountered Gandhi as an antidote to the deep critiques of Marx and Nietzsche. By September 1951, King was twenty two years old, a young adult entering a PhD program at Boston University. He was ready for greater refinement, depth, and elegance in his intellectual system. During this period he continued to worship and preach in churches, learning from some of America's best preachers and orators while also developing interracial friendships.

In 1954 Paul Tillich wrote a book that refuted Nietzsche's critique of Christian love as a glorification of weakness: *Love, Power, and Justice: Ontological Analyses and Ethical Applications.* King knew about ethical applications of love from his parents, church members, and all of the people who lived the Christian faith in a racist society. But this ontological perspective on love was a new and much needed extension of thought.

What did King learn from Tillich? We know that he learned a great deal from Gandhi, but what did he need from Tillich? After all, when it came time to write his dissertation at Boston University, he did not write about Gandhi but rather about Paul Tillich. Tillich believed that love has within it a special capacity, a mysterious power, the ability to suffer and to forgive for the benefit of others, the common good. As Tillich writes in 1951 in his magisterial two-volume *Systematic Theology*:

> All love, except agape, is dependent on contingent characteristics which change and are partial, such as repulsion and attraction, passion and sympathy. Agape is independent of these states. It affirms the other unconditionally. It is agape that suffers and forgives. It seeks the personal fulfillment of the other.[23]

King yearned for formal and rigorous intellectual presentations of these ideas, and he found some of this in Tillich. In 1963, as he sat in a Birmingham jail cell, alone and without paper, without books, without a pen (before his lawyer could smuggle in a newspaper and a pen) King had only himself, his education, his breadth and depth of learning, his memory, and his imagination to draw from. But he did have an ensemble of formidable internal conversation partners—beginning with Jesus and his parental role models, and including Thoreau, Mays, Gandhi, Thurman, and Tillich—helping him to think about the nature of love, power, and justice.

I summarize the key elements of Tillich's perspective on the three concepts expressed in *Love, Power, and Justice* in this way:

- Love is the drive for the unity of the separated. Love manifests its greatest power where it overcomes the greatest separation.

---

[23] Paul Tillich, *Systematic Theology,* vol. 1: *Reason and Revelation; Being and God* (Chicago: University of Chicago Press, 1973), 116.

- Power is the drive to actualize potential (potency) against the counter force of negation.
- Justice is establishing and preserving the order that love seeks in reuniting that which is separated. Justice should and must be creative and adaptive as it requires love's reuniting, restorative energy to fulfill itself.
- Justice establishes a new base line in social reality. But love transcends justice, aims higher, and reaches farther, and thereby fulfills justice.

Against Nietzsche, Tillich proclaimed that love should be the foundation of power, and that Christian love must be united with power in order to accomplish its twofold goal of negating what is against love and of saving the souls of those who act against love.[24]

King understood that power was fundamentally the focus of politics. One of the early fathers of political science, Harold Lasswell, in 1936 defined politics as "the art of who gets what, when, and how."[25] Since my days as a political science major at Morehouse,[26] I have admired the simplicity and clarity of Lasswell's focus on politics as a distributional team sport. During my time at Harvard Divinity School, I heard Julian Bond speak at Harvard Law School, where he revised Lasswell to define his own profession as one concerned with "who gets how much of what, from whom, when, where and how."[27] I admire two additional definitions, one from the California social psychologist Wade Nobles, who says power is "the ability to define reality and to have others respond to your

---

[24] John J. Ansbro, *Martin Luther King, Jr: The Making of a Mind* (Maryknoll, NY: Orbis Books, 1984), 8.

[25] Harold Lasswell, *Politics: Who Gets What, When, How* (New York: McGraw Hill, 1936).

[26] Dr. Robert Brisbane, Dr. Abraham Davis, and Dr. Tobe Johnson were among the leading thinkers in the political science department over many decades.

[27] Julian Bond, lecture, Harvard Law School (c. 1978).

reality as if it were your own."[28] And there is the priceless definition attributed to comedian Groucho Marx: "Politics is the art of
looking for trouble, finding it everywhere, diagnosing it incorrectly,
and applying the wrong remedies."[29]

Indeed, King understood that oppressed and excluded people
need political goods like voting, running for office, governing, and
making policy to truly participate in democracy.[30] By the early 1960s,
he expanded from political goods to economic goods. The March
on Washington in 1963 was billed as a march for jobs and freedom.
It did not help to have the right to sit anywhere on a desegregated
bus but not have the money to pay the fare or have a job to ride to.

In 1968, King defined power as "the ability to achieve purpose
. . . the strength required to bring about social, political or economic changes." And he insisted that law be wedded to a "new kind
of power—power infused with love and justice."[31] Christian ethicist
Timothy P. Jackson writes: "To the end of his life, King continued
to believe in the project of marrying American law with biblical morality. Put less pointedly, he steadfastly refused to segregate
positive law (acts actually on the books) from natural law (timeless
dictates of a good conscience) and eternal law (the will of God)."[32]

In going into this phase of King's life in some detail, I am attempting to illustrate how the moral leader must develop clarity

---

[28] Wade Nobles, "Critical Ideas and Concepts," www.drwadenobles.com.
This website contains the definition and other resources. Nobles is professor
emeritus of Africana studies and black psychology at San Francisco State University.

[29] In Bennett Cerf, *Try and Stop Me* (New York: Simon and Schuster, 1944).

[30] For a theory about categories of goods that justice and politics are
concerned to distribute fairly, see William Galston, *Justice and the Human Good*
(Chicago: University of Chicago Press, 1980). Galston served as domestic policy
adviser in the Clinton administration.

[31] Martin Luther King Jr., *Where Do We Go From Here: Chaos or Community?*
(Boston: Beacon Press, 2010), 37, 66.

[32] Timothy Jackson, *Political Agape: Christian Love and Liberal Democracy*
(Grand Rapids, MI: Eerdmans, 2015), 400.

about the moral life and the just society. That process can involve existential crisis and emotional anguish. But in addition to being students of the moral life and just society, moral leaders move from thought to action as they *frame issues as moral issues that invite people and compel moral action.*

In addition to being students of the moral life (what they think), moral leaders also undertake four critical practices (what they do). Moral leaders:

- frame issues as moral issues and communicate in ways that invite;
- strive to live an exemplary life, engaging in exemplary actions but undaunted by failure;
- invest in the next generation by building enduring institutions; and
- having done their best in life, aim to teach others how to die a good death.

Moral Leaders Frame Issues as Moral Issues

In this capacity the moral leader becomes a public intellectual and a public voice. Moral leaders as public moralists or public intellectuals think and communicate ideas strategically to recalibrate the moral compass of the nation and to catalyze constructive action.

That's what I think, but what do others think about the vocation and work of public intellectuals? In an influential essay titled "The Responsibility of Intellectuals," America's preeminent public intellectual Noam Chomsky writes: "Intellectuals are in a position to expose the lies of governments, to analyze actions according to their causes and motives and often hidden intentions. They have the power that comes from political liberty, access to information and freedom of expression."[33]

I believe that we need preachers and pastors to become more intentional as local leaders who think in public, who think and communicate from the pulpit, particularly in light of two trends: (1) high rates of biblical illiteracy in the culture, and (2) a growing culture of anti-intellectualism and mistrust of science, reason, and data.

Ed Stetzer writes: "Pew Research tells us that 23 percent of Americans didn't read a single book in the last year. That's three times the number who didn't read a book in 1978. Whether it's the Internet, video games, the TV or increased time spent on entertainment and sports, Americans are spending less time between the pages of any book, not just the Good Book."[34]

"A recent LifeWay Research study found that only 45 percent of those who regularly attend church read the Bible more than once a week. Over 40 percent of the people attending are reading their Bibles occasionally—maybe once or twice a month, if at all. In fact, 18 percent of attenders say they never read the Bible."[35] That means there are millions of North Americans who lack meaningful awareness and knowledge of religious ideas, symbols, and ethical teaching; the historical importance of the Bible as a decisive force in generating Western civilization; and its salience as a masterpiece of literature and language.

With respect to anti-intellectualism, Janice Gross Stein, a Canadian public intellectual, notes the dumbing down of public discussion in contemporary democratic societies. "Without a well-informed citizenry," she writes, "vigorously debating the future, our democratic institutions atrophy, becoming the preserve of a political

---

[33] Noam Chomsky, "The Responsibility of Intellectuals," *The New York Review of Books* (February 23, 1967).

[34] Ed Stetzer, "Biblical Illiteracy by the Numbers: Part 1: The Challenge," *Christianity Today* (October 17, 2014); for updated statistics, see Andrew Perrin, "Who Doesn't Read Books in America?" Factank: News in the Numbers, Pew Research Center (September 20, 2019).

[35] Stetzer, "Biblical Illiteracy by the Numbers."

class and privileged elites. Our public space empties out and private interest replaces public concerns and a shared sense of a common future and the collective good."[36]

Together with what the Pew Research Center and other researchers have reported in recent years about decline in many mainline Protestant, Catholic, and evangelical traditions, we should realize there may be an opportunity lurking here for public moralists and intellectuals to fill some of this vacuum and recalibrate our moral compass. As Nelson Wiseman notes, "The public intellectual taps and channels the critical, contemplative and creative sides of his audience's minds."[37]

Moral leaders have an opportunity to communicate their values and visions in the public square. Integrity, courage, and imagination play a critical role in legitimizing a leader. The communication landscape of modern culture is evolving rapidly. In the past, men created and controlled access to the conventional communication channels of print, radio and television. With social and technological changes under way, nearly everyone has access to channels of public communication. During King's era, and in Jewish and Christian America, the preacher and rabbi were the authoritative interpreters and messengers of truth. King was one of the best preachers of the twentieth century, and his gifts for how to say things well were matched by the substance of what he had to say and bolstered by the life he was compelled to live as a global symbol of the civil rights movement. Even as the culture moves beyond formal proclamation as a primary way of transmitting ideas, it is useful to appreciate this art form; it will never disappear, given the human love of rhetoric and real-time poetic speech.

I want to interweave the role and opportunities of the prophet and preacher with these understandings of public intellectualism.

---

[36] Janice Gross Stein, "What Are Public Intellectuals For?" in *The Public Intellectual in Canada*, ed. Nelson Wiseman (Toronto: University of Toronto Press, 2013), 16.

[37] Wiseman, *The Public Intellectual in Canada*, 4.

As I do so, I introduce a counter narrative about what preachers should be thinking and talking about. From the Hebrew prophets to the early Christian preachers, their priority was to pay careful attention to the immediate situation in life. They were shepherds called to attend to local knowledge, experience, and practice. They talked often about mundane things. But as they did so, they connected the local to the larger, grander themes of God's profound concern for all of creation and all of God's children. Perhaps the bumper sticker puts it aptly: *Think globally, act locally.* While that gets close to capturing my point, my preferred bumper sticker reads: *Jesus is coming soon. . . . Look busy.*

Note the interplay and dialectic between the grand and the mundane.

In his 1962 classic *The Prophets* Abraham Joshua Heschel writes about the viewpoint of the prophet:

> What manner of man is the prophet? A student of philosophy who turns from the discourses of the great metaphysicians to the orations of the prophets may feel as if he were going from the realm of the sublime to an area of trivialities. Instead of dealing with the timeless issues of being and becoming, of matter and form, of definitions and demonstrations, he is thrown into orations about widows and orphans, about the corruption of judges and the affairs of the marketplace. Instead of showing us a way through the mansions of the mind, the prophets take us to the slums. The world is a proud place, full of beauty, but the prophets are scandalized, and rave as if the whole world were a slum. They make much ado about paltry things, lavishing excessive language upon trifling subjects.[38]

Many people who have endured poor quality sermons or speeches can attest to how these speakers often "make much ado

---

[38] Abraham J. Heschel, *The Prophets* (New York: Harper Torchbooks, 1962).

about paltry things, lavishing excessive language upon trifling sub-jects," but that is not the compliment implied in Heschel's charac-terization. Indeed, Heschel reminds us that the prophets used the mundane instances of everyday life to amplify larger ethical and even metaphysical truths.

Let us shift now from the identity and vocation of the moral leader as public intellectual to the tasks, practices, and teachable arts.

Stated directly, moral leaders—whether speaking as public moral-ists, public intellectuals, prophets, or preachers—*(1) address the grand questions of human existence and ultimate concern by (2) providing compel-ling responses to those grand questions (3) directed to the public at large, (4) in short (brief or digestible) form, (5) with the goal of catalyzing strategic ethical action.* This is a time when moral imagination comes into play.

They frame the grand questions of human existence and ultimate concern.

Moral leaders can start with parochial issues and re-contextualize them into a larger moral drama that invites everyone's attention and interest. Dr. King did this as he took the issue of desegregating the buses in Montgomery, Alabama, after Rosa Parks's deliberate and defiant moral agency in transgressing segregation laws, and he placed it into the long arc of conflict between good and evil. Many people outside of Alabama wouldn't have been able to find Mont-gomery on a map or recall if they had ever heard of it (although it was one of the capital cities of the Confederacy and thereafter capital of Alabama).

King made Montgomery a global stage for the moral drama of good and evil. But a leader can work from the other direction. That is, leaders can begin with a large and general issue and then funnel down into a particular issue. For instance, one could begin speaking about the dangers of Artificial Intelligence (AI) and its impacts on human relationships, and then pivot from that general concern to the local context of how each of us relates to our mobile phone. Whether one moves from the particular to the universal or from the universal to the particular, the responsibility is to frame issues as moral issues. For many issues people can perceive and make judgments about what is right and wrong, good and bad, and praiseworthy and blameworthy. But as Harvard Business School professor Joseph Badaracco observes, the hard decisions "are often matters of right versus right, not right versus wrong."[39] That is, when competing good and right options arise, we may face greater anxiety about how to decide.

Currently, our public square is dominated by people who make strong, unqualified, declarative statements. This is most evident among national and local politicians, religious leaders, and media pundits. They come in conservative and liberal versions. I cringe to hear them make unsubstantiated claims and stake out uncompromising positions. A moral leader adds to our public life by framing large and difficult questions in a way that invites reflection, critical examination of evidence, and consideration of the common good. One thinks of Dr. King's final book title, *Where Do We Go from Here: Chaos or Community?* Indeed, his question could serve as a helpful exercise for any group that must deliberate about its future.

They provide compelling responses to those same grand questions.

They do not seek to answer large questions, as if such questions can be settled once and for all. Rather, they seek to offer responses. New Testament scholar Gail O'Day says that the Bible, especially the Wisdom literature (Psalms, Proverbs, Ecclesiastes, Song of Solomon, Lamentations) raises grand questions about human existence: Why do the good die young? Why do bad things happen to good people? What becomes of the soul after death? How can belief and doubt coexist constructively? She says there is no "answer" to such questions. But there is a reply, restated throughout the Hebrew Bible and the New Testament. Simply, you are not alone as you

---

[39] Joseph Badaracco, *Defining Moments: When Managers Must Choose between Right and Right* (Boston: Harvard Business School Press, 1997), 1.

face this crisis. God (Yahweh) declares, "I will be with you."[40] At a time when people of conscience often feel alone or outnumbered, it can be a great source of comfort to be reminded that they are not alone. For those who do not accept theistic formulations of this assurance, we can assure them of human solidarity and community.

They address the public at large, all rational people, not simply their own tribe.

This is part of the project of serving the common good. Public intellectuals speak to the people, all people. The act of addressing the people contributes to a vivid sense of the common good and its possibilities. Speech can help constitute community. They resist the temptation to sing only the familiar hymns to and with their familiar friends. They seek to de-parochialize every text by asking, How can we be radically inclusive? Who is not at this table?

They communicate in short form.

This is subjective and perhaps controversial, but the op-ed essay, concise radio commentary, and the brief sermon seem to be the most adequate genre for our age. Shakespeare told us that "brevity is the soul of wit." In being concise lies our salvation. Get to the point, please. Have something to say, say it well, say it briefly, and close (or "slam shut"). This seems especially well suited for our attention deficit audiences, twitter media culture, and even heads of state who are suspicious of extended, coherent sentences. Finally,

They seek to catalyze strategic ethical action.

Having framed the moral dimensions of a significant issue and offering possible responses to a broad rational public in short form, the moral leader is then challenged to invite people and invite action. Invitations come in many forms, and all of them seem to be effective. Flash mobs have been mobilized to help people, bear

---

[40] Gail O'Day, sermon, Emory University, 1996.

witness to certain issues, and bring people together in community who might otherwise have remained separate and atomized. Often people are waiting for a call to action. One of the deans of homiletics, Henry Mitchell, says that every sermon should invite, or prescribe, a behavioral response. The antiphonal structure of the I-Thou, divine-human encounter denotes that every call demands a response. Public intellectuals invite people to action. From ideas and language to reflection, decision, and action.

In light of these criteria and insights, let us broaden the focus to look at Reinhold Niebuhr and Dolores Huerta as moral leaders and public intellectuals.

Reinhold Niebuhr

The ethicist and Niebuhr biographer Larry Rasmussen begins his book by observing:

> When Harvard University sought a keynote speaker for its 350th anniversary celebration in 1986, an occasion which called for a public intellectual with a commanding presence who could speak across the disciplines, American literature professor Alan Heimert told President Bok that only two people in the last twenty years could have made that speech— Walter Lippmann and Reinhold Niebuhr—and they were both gone.[41]

He continues:

> Reinhold Niebuhr was a dramatist of theological ideas in the public arena and, with the exception of Martin Luther King, Jr., commanded more influence than any other 20th century theologian and preacher in the United States. He

---

[41] Larry Rasmussen, ed., *Reinhold Niebuhr: Theologian of Public Life* (Minneapolis: Fortress, 1991), 1.

was, remarkably, a public theologian in a nation not much given to theological reflection on its considerable power in the world, nor generative of intellectuals as common fixtures of public life.

Niebuhr was a public intellectual and enjoyed it, an activist-scholar held in high respect in his culture who nonetheless cultivated a stance of sharp, independent criticism. He was, in fact, a prophet heard in the king's chapel and the king's court, chastising the certitudes of a confident culture and exposing its fault lines with rhetorical power and the sheer force of his personality. . . .

If recognized as a prophetic voice and a public intellectual, Niebuhr demurred from 'theologian' as the proper title for the trade he plied.[42]

(Karl Paul) Reinhold Niebuhr was born in 1892 in Missouri, the son of a German Evangelical Synod pastor. He declared his wish to become a minister in 1906 and was instructed in Greek by his father. Niebuhr recalled of his father, "I was thrilled by his sermons and regarded him as the most interesting man in town." After Eden Seminary and Yale Divinity School, where he wrote a thesis in 1914 titled "The Validity and Certainty of Religious Knowledge," he began a thirteen-year tenure as pastor of Bethel Evangelical Church in Detroit. There he kept a diary that formed the basis of his wonderful little book *Leaves from the Notebook of a Tamed Cynic*.

Although Niebuhr became the most powerful public intellectual and Christian preacher of his time, he did not start that way. He grew, and he evolved. Rasmussen says, "The play of Niebuhr's mind was most evident when he preached. Here, Niebuhr the dramatist of theological ideas for public life was perhaps most at home. His sermons were usually given with a few spare notes, or none at all. Some were reworked for publication as 'sermonic essays,' however."[43]

---

[42] Ibid.
[43] Ibid.

In the first year of his ministry in Detroit (1915), Niebuhr writes:

There is something ludicrous about a callow young fool like myself standing up to preach a sermon to these good folks. I talk wisely about life and know little about life's problems. I tell them of the need of sacrifice, although most of them could tell me something about what that really means.

Now that I have preached about a dozen sermons I find I am repeating myself. A different text simply means a different pretext for saying the same thing over again. The few ideas that I had worked into sermons at the seminary have all been used, and now what?[44]

Then, in words that are amusingly prophetic in light of his subsequent extraordinary influence, he writes:

I suppose that as the years go by, life and experience will prompt some new ideas and I will find some in the Bible that I have missed so far. . . .

You are supposed to stand before a congregation, brimming over with a great message. Here I am trying to find a new little message each Sunday. If I really had great convictions, I suppose they would struggle for birth each week. As the matter stands, *I struggle to find an idea worth presenting* and I almost dread the approach of a new Sabbath. I don't know whether I can ever accustom myself to the task of bringing light and inspiration in regular weekly installments.

How in the world can you reconcile the inevitability of Sunday and its task with the moods and caprices of the soul? *The prophet speaks only when he is inspired.* The parish preacher must speak whether he is inspired or not. I wonder whether it

---

[44] Reinhold Niebuhr, *Leaves from the Notebook of a Tamed Cynic*, pbk. ed. (Louisville, KY: Westminster John Knox Press, 1990), 9.

is possible to live on a high enough plane to do that without sinning against the Holy Spirit (my emphasis).[45]

He left that parish in 1928 and was appointed Dodge Professor in Applied Christianity at Union Theological Seminary in 1930. In 1939 he delivered the Gifford Lectures in Edinburgh even as Nazi bombing occurred. War and suffering transformed and radicalized his theology and preaching. During those years he spoke of human pride, of creating peace by balancing power among superpowers, and the many expressions of arrogance that offend God's creative intent such as nuclear weapons, racism, genocide, sexism, and so on. Ten years later, by virtue of his writings and sermons, he was asked by the State Department to advise on policy in Europe. Ironically, this dangerous prophet was also being monitored by the FBI.

Niebuhr wrote long, complicated books, classics like *Moral Man and Immoral Society* and *The Nature and Destiny of Man,* and he admitted that his brother Helmut Richard was a better, clearer writer. But in his sermons and his articles in the magazine *Christianity and Crisis* and other publications he arrested the attention of the wider public. His sermons were published under the title *Beyond Tragedy.* In 1964, as his health was failing, he received the Presidential Medal of Freedom. He also wrote to Dr. King in 1965 to express regret that he could not join him for the march from Selma to Montgomery due to a serious illness.

Niebuhr's familiar serenity prayer may very well be the best symbol of public theology in user-friendly form:

> God grant me the serenity
> to accept the things I cannot change;
> courage to change the things I can;
> and wisdom to know the difference.
> > Amen.

---

45 Ibid., 12.

Niebuhr's prayer was embraced by Alcoholics Anonymous in 1941 and has touched and helped millions of people. Niebuhr was a public intellectual who addressed the grand topics of human existence. He addressed the grand questions of human existence and ultimate concern by providing compelling responses to those grand questions directed to the public at large, in short form, with the goal of catalyzing strategic ethical action. In fact, he did this so well that his own government became suspicious of him. He struggled to find his voice as a young preacher and pastor but, as his diary indicates, world events compelled him to notice the impact on the lives of the people of Bethel Church. He commented on local things like the marketing and cost of new Ford automobiles that his parishioners desired. But he pivoted to link that to the corrosive effects of capitalism that drive humans to place material things above human dignity and worth. This could be called the prophetic pivot.

Dolores Huerta

Reflecting on her early life in California, and the influence of her mother on her own development, Dolores Huerta observed that her mother was a "Mexican American Horatio Alger type" who pushed her "to get involved in all these youth activities. . . . We took violin lessons. I took piano lessons. I took dancing lessons. I belonged to the church choir. . . . And I was a very active Girl Scout from the time I was eight to the time I was eighteen."[46]

Because her mother worked constantly, she and the other children were often cared for by relatives, especially her grandfather. Biographer Stacey Sowards observes that in doing so, her mother modeled for the children a "reversal of traditional gendered caretaker roles" that encouraged independent and assertive female leadership.[47] "Huerta's grandfather called her Seven Tongues, because

---

[46] Margaret Rose, "Dolores Huerta: The United Farm Workers Union," in *The Human Tradition in American Labor History*, ed. Eric Arnesen (Wilmington, DE: Scholarly Resources, 2004), 217.

[47] Sowards, *Sí, Ella Puede!*, 36.

she talked so much and with great ease, foreshadowing her assertive persona as an adult.[48] She was reared in the diverse city of Stockton, California, where Chinese, Latinos, Native Americans, African Americans, Japanese, Italians, and others lived in close proximity. She attended the University of the Pacific's Stockton College where she earned a teaching certificate. These were years framed by the Great Depression and World War II.[49]

She often experienced the tension among her obligation to her family, traditional Catholic family norms, and her sense of vocation as a social justice activist with and for farmworkers. She experienced two divorces, and she and her third romantic companion, Raymond Chavez (brother of Cesar), never married, although they had two children together (bringing the total to eleven).

Most relevant for our purposes, when Dolores stood to speak, one could hear and feel a power and authority that few other grassroots leaders possessed. While Cesar Chavez, her mentor and the more famous icon, helped to organize and mobilize the masses, Huerta, who was better educated, spoke eloquently with the love and pain of a mother (some called it "militant motherhood"), all the while framing issues in a moral way and inviting people to join. I quote her at length here to illustrate her remarkable rhetorical power. She also offers a perspective on love, power, and justice, most of it implicit rather than explicit. Speaking in 1974 at Stanford University, she said:

> What I'd like to tell people that we're no longer asking anybody for charity. We're not saying to people, "Well, please help the poor farmworkers." . . . *Chale* [no way] on that. No more of that. But we say to people now—You have a responsibility to farmworkers, because the farmworkers feed you. A farmworker puts food on your table every single day. And so you have a responsibility, so we ask you just to do a very simple thing. Fast! Don't eat lettuce. Don't eat grapes. Don't drink wine. That's a simple thing for people to do. Just don't eat those three things.

---

[48] Ibid.
[49] Ibid., 38.

Then we ask people to help picket. Well that's a little harder. Some people will say, "Well that's not my bag." Picketing is passé. People don't do that anymore. What is picketing? Picketing is just walking, just like a *peregrinación*. You know what a *peregrinación* is—a pilgrimage. You're walking because you're walking for justice. And when people say to you that they don't want to walk, remind them that a farmworker has to walk thousands of miles in his lifetime to feed you. And when he walks he doesn't walk straight up—he has to bend over like a hairpin when he's thinning, when he's cutting the lettuce, when he's cutting the celery, when he's picking tomatoes. He's bent over. And that's the way he's got to do it 8, 9, 10 hours when he's picking cucumbers. Tell people that, and when they're picking grapes or onions a farmworker has to walk on his knees. So tell people that if we ask them to come out and join us for a couple of hours on Friday and Saturday, that's nothing compared to what a farmworker has to go through to put food on their table. He has to work out in the heat, he has to work out there in the cold.[50]

Huerta proved to be a compelling lay preacher who could educate and inspire a crowd to the point of strategic action.

Cesar Chavez and Dolores Huerta

[50] Ibid., 115–16.

Moral Leaders Engage in Exemplary Action
Undaunted by Failure

Returning to King, by virtue of his skill as a communicator King's presence became an event. He was frequently arrested, and he sometimes wrote communications while incarcerated. But going to jail in Birmingham and writing his letter from the jail raised this to a new level.

Imagine that you have engaged in civil disobedience for an issue of justice that is important to you. You have been arrested and placed in a jail cell alone for three days. Some local leaders have posted a message on Facebook and the local online newspaper questioning your rationale for breaking the law and urging you to obey the law. You have only a pen and a pad of paper—no books, no digital devices, no other resources. What would you write in response to your critics?

In the extraordinary letter King wrote from jail we see how he, as a moral leader, drew on his understanding of the moral life and just society, and specifically Gandhi and Tillich to persuade the religious leaders and communities, the public at large, on grand questions such as the problem with human nature, finitude, and sin. He writes:

> Paul Tillich has said that sin is separation. Isn't segregation an existential expression of man's tragic separation, his awful estrangement, his terrible sinfulness? Thus, it is that I can urge men to obey the 1954 decision of the Supreme Court, for it is morally right; and I can urge them to disobey segregation ordinances, for they are morally wrong.[51]

King also countered the authors' chidings by expressing candidly his own disappointments:

---

[51] Martin Luther King Jr., "Letter from Birmingham Jail" (April 16, 1963), The Estate of Martin Luther King Jr., www.kingpapers.org.

I had hoped that the white moderate would see this need. Perhaps I was too optimistic; perhaps I expected too much. I suppose I should have realized that few members of the oppressor race can understand the deep groans and passionate yearnings of the oppressed race, and still fewer have the vision to see that injustice must be rooted out by strong, persistent and determined action. I am thankful, however, that some of our white brothers in the South have grasped the meaning of this social revolution and committed themselves to it. They are still too few in quantity, but they are big in quality. Some—such as Ralph McGill, Lillian Smith, Harry Golden, James McBride Dabbs, Ann Braden, and Sarah Patton Boyle—have written about our struggle in eloquent and prophetic terms. Others have marched with us down nameless streets of the South.

Let me take note of my other major disappointment. I have been so greatly disappointed with the white church and its leadership. Of course, there are some notable exceptions. I am not unmindful of the fact that each of you has taken some significant stands on this issue. I commend you, Reverend Stallings, for your Christian stand on this past Sunday, in welcoming Negroes to your worship service on a non segregated basis. I commend the Catholic leaders of this state for integrating Spring Hill College several years ago.[52]

As a former institutional president, I was pleased to note that he commends a college for asserting its moral leadership, and he affirms the courage of white allies. He continues:

In spite of my shattered dreams, I came to Birmingham with the hope that the white religious leadership of this community would see the justice of our cause and, with deep moral concern, would serve as the channel through which

---

[52] Ibid.

our just grievances could reach the power structure. I had hoped that each of you would understand. But again I have been disappointed.[53]

King also reminds us of his frustrated expectations that white church leaders would emerge as moral leaders amid the social crises of their time:

In deep disappointment I have wept over the laxity of the church. But be assured that my tears have been tears of love. There can be no deep disappointment where there is not deep love. Yes, I love the church. How could I do otherwise? I am in the rather unique position of being the son, the grandson and the great grandson of preachers. Yes, I see the church as the body of Christ. But, oh! How we have blemished and scarred that body through social neglect and through fear of being nonconformists. . . .

But the judgment of God is upon the church as never before. If today's church does not recapture the sacrificial spirit of the early church, it will lose its authenticity, forfeit the loyalty of millions, and be dismissed as an irrelevant social club with no meaning for the twentieth century. Every day I meet young people whose disappointment with the church has turned into outright disgust.[54]

King's letter was a sharp scold to moderate religious leaders. And he put religious communities on notice. If you stand with the political status quo and legitimize its injustices and oppression then you will experience decline and irrelevance, or what King called "the judgment of God," which was also the judgment of good and decent people.

---

[53] Ibid.
[54] Ibid.

We could conclude that sitting in the Birmingham jail unjustly, King decided not to keep silent but to protest through, as they said of Winston Churchill, "weaponizing the English language."[55] He was able to imagine and think and write this way because enduring institutions had invested in him.

In addition to his willingness to be arrested for his values, King sought to live a simple life, one that did not aim to accumulate excessive wealth or material assets. He was committed to a mindful possession of his few possessions. Whenever I travel through International Terminal E of Atlanta's William B. Hartsfield/Maynard H. Jackson Airport, I smile to see some of King's possessions on display for the world to see. His suit, bible, reading glasses, clergy robe, copy of his Nobel Prize medallion, and his briefcase are there as quiet reminders of a well-lived life. When he died, he did not have large savings or investments. He wanted to avoid public and media scrutiny of his lifestyle, but he also wanted to model for his peer and later leaders the importance of a simple life of dignity, service, and sacrifice.

I have suggested that moral leaders live and lead with integrity, courage and imagination as they serve the common good and invite others to join them. In doing so, they think about substantive matters like the relation of love, power, and justice and how to effect social change. They are students of the moral life and think through the moral options for making decisions and shaping action. Moral leaders communicate effectively to frame moral issues and invite action. They speak truth to power, and they speak power to the powerless. They strive to live exemplary lives but are not daunted by their shortcomings. They accept that they are not perfect.

Consider the process of qualifying, disqualifying, and requalifying for moral leadership. In my study and observation of moral leadership, I think that there are distinct phases of awareness along the way to becoming a moral leader. How do people qualify?

---

[55] "The Darkest Hour," a film about Winston Churchill during World War II.

Service

In most instances the journey from agency to leadership seems to begin with service. Service is a decentering activity in which the needs of others become one's priority. Those who serve others wisely understand their aim to be empowering others toward self-efficacy and, when possible, self-determination and self-sufficiency. They do so out of respect for the autonomy of others. And they seek to avoid cultivating dependency and codependency. Service should offer immediate and direct alleviation of misery and deprivation.

Sacrifice

At times service leads to a deeper sense of empathy and identification with the one who journeys forward. Service invites sacrifice, sometimes in increasing amounts. Sacrifice is a more profound expression of privileging others' needs. In sacrificing for others, we accept that the act of renunciation can be purifying. We can live on less and in sharing our lives become more authentic. We recognize that we have enough already. No one can decide the degree of our sacrifice because no one knows when we feel the pinch of depleting resources, security, energy, and time. But sacrifice is a quiet demonstration of deepening commitment to the empowerment of others.

During the early years of organizing farmworkers to demand their civil rights and resist exploitation by wealthy growers in California, Dolores Huerta wrote to Cesar Chavez of numerous personal sacrifices for the cause:

> Yes, I am still breathing, although I got a bad scare last week. I kept feeling worse and worse so I went to the County Hospital and hey [sic] shook me up because they said I have to have an operation. . . . I have a tumor in one of my ovaries. . . . The only reason I hate to get operated on is because I

hate to lose the time. My health, plus no bay [*sic*] sitter is one of the reasons things hav [*sic*] not been moving, so help me Cesar, without someone to watch my kids, i [*sic*] just can't find enough time to work, especially in the evening when it counts. . . . Also, my finances have been terrible. [56]

Struggle

Some people feel called even further along the journey to engage in struggle. Often struggle emerges from a recognition that personal, individual, or retail interventions cannot match the magnitude of the problem that crushes other lives. When systems and policies and laws and budgets and power structures and cultures must be dismantled for the sake of the common good, we are called to struggle. The greatest moral leaders—Gandhi, Chavez, Baker, Huerta, King, and others—led people in nonviolent struggles for change and sought to redress past harms to innocent people by appealing to a larger public sense of morality, decency, and human empathy. They did not desire to see anger channeled into violent action. Sigmund Freud said that "civilization began the first time an angry person cast a word instead of a rock."[57] Other moral leaders like Nelson Mandela and Malcolm X found their way to nonviolence through advocating a more aggressive approach of self defense and, when justified, tactical violence to compromise the ability of opponents to do further harm.

Suffering

As I have observed and experienced this continuum of ethical commitment, the experience of suffering for a righteous cause is an

---

[56] Sowards, *Sí, Ella Puede!*, 70.

[57] The saying appeared in an 1893 article published by Freud and Josef Breuer, "Ueber den psychischen Mechanismus hysterischer Phänomene" [On the psychical mechanism of hysterical phenomena] in a Vienna medical journal.

inevitable element of change-affecting struggles. People may experience inconvenience and pain in the process of serving and sacrificing; it is almost inevitable amid struggle. Although the mother of eleven children, farmworker activist Dolores Huerta took a vow of poverty, which often caused piercing pain and micro-humiliations as she sought to provide for her kids. Each day she sought confirmation or a sign from God that this was morally proper. At one point she admits:

> I didn't have money to buy my daughter Celeste shoes for her confirmation and so she had these white shoes [that] were all torn with holes on them . . . and I see Celeste coming down the aisle with her torn tennis shoes and I'm kind of flinching, and just behind her, there's several farm worker children that are coming down the aisle with torn tennis shoes and to me that was a sign.[58]

Some might consider the inner pain of a mother who could not provide new shoes and protect her child from the taunts of her peers as a form of suffering. Others might prefer to reserve the term for more extreme moral misery and punishment. Later we say more about how moral leaders teach us to die with dignity and grace. Such deaths include the very personal experience of emotional and physical anguish, profound loss, and wrenching pain. As I write this, I have in mind the images of Robert F. Kennedy, Malcolm X, and Martin Luther King Jr. lying on the floor with bullets in their bodies. Suffering and anguish bathed in blood for a cause greater than their own status, prosperity, or pleasure. Those disturbing images of leaders in suits covered in blood always prompt the clarifying question, *For what cause are you willing to suffer?*

In my view, beyond service, sacrifice, struggle, and suffering is the most profound form of leadership, generosity, and generativity that takes the form of what philosophers call supererogation, that

---

[58] Sowards, *Sí, Ella Puede!*, 109.

is, the act that is beyond obligation Supererogation may involve ultimate risk to one's own safety and personhood.

Supererogation

When we risk our life while saving the life of another, we move beyond duty to self-sacrificing love, what New Testament scholars call agapic love. Philosophers draw the line on what is morally required of us—the scope of moral requirement—at different points. I think that it is desirable to increase the incentives and public recognition for good deeds done, especially across various demographic and political dividing lines.[59]

For most moral leaders, service, sacrifice and struggle are sufficient to qualify for moral leadership.

Disqualification

Obviously, leaders can be disqualified for any deliberate and intentional violation or breach of the moral order and trust. The scandals that disqualify illustrate how a lifetime of qualifying can be nullified in moments. I think that the greatest challenge in disqualification pertains to the ecology of trust and how it is perceived by those involved. Can we understand what happened to this leader? Is this disqualification of an anomalous, singular, episodic and temporary nature or is it a more profound and long-lasting disabling condition? Not "should we" but "can we" forgive the leader? And, when appropriate, does the community perceive that the leader demonstrates the requisite self-awareness, humility to request forgiveness, remorse, brokenness of spirit and sincerity to begin rebuilding trust? These sensitive processes take time and require enormous investment in a culture of reform and repair.

---

[59] Cheshire Calhoun, ed., *Setting the Moral Compass: Essays by Women Philosophers* (Oxford: Oxford University Press, 2004), 72–112.

Requalifying

There can be life and service after a fall. We have observed this in the lives of many leaders who swore to uphold the public trust—from Congressman Adam Clayton Powell and Mayor Marion Barry to evangelist Jimmy Swaggart, General David Petraeus, and attorney Eliott Spitzer. Even nonmoral leaders like golf champion Tiger Woods demonstrate America's willingness to welcome admired prodigal sons and daughters back home. As for requalifying, we all fall, and most of us get back up. In *A Farewell to Arms* Hemingway writes: "The world breaks everyone and afterward many are strong at the broken places." Leaders can requalify through a long patient journey that includes daily remorse, self-examination and self-criticism, acts of mercy and service, trusting that they can change, and living with gratitude that each day in the sunshine makes them healthier. At the end of the long journey the community determines whether or not fallen leaders return to more conscientious level of service and self-denial. Leaders don't get to put themselves back on the team or back on the field.

Obviously, as with Dr. King, all of this becomes more complicated when dealing with a historical figure who is no longer here to do the work of soul repair and reconciliation with victims. But from a certain theological point of view, one can imagine that King is paying reparations and making amends in the Promised Land.

When good and decent leaders experience failure and disappointment and admit their problems and seek help, then we can respect and empathize with their struggles and their journey toward wholeness and health.

In a televised conversation on CNN, November 15, 2017, I suggested that Judge Roy Moore, a candidate for the US Senate from Alabama, should not be rewarded with the privilege of serving due to the many unresolved allegations of inappropriate sexual communication with minors.[60] I suggested to host Don Lemon and other

---

[60] CNN "Tonight with Don Lemon," guest, November 15, 2017.

guests that Judge Moore should first engage in soul repair (dealing with his issues and beginning the road to healing and self care) before moving to moral repair, which would include admitting his wrongdoing, apologizing to the women, and seeking forgiveness and possible reconciliation. When leaders are unwilling to do this themselves, they may need an intervention by more objective and spiritually mature friends and family. The New Testament offers one approach to this in Galatians:

> My friends, if anyone is detected in a transgression, you who have received the Spirit should restore such a one in a spirit of gentleness. Take care that you yourselves are not tempted. Bear one another's burdens, and in this way you will fulfill the law of Christ. For if those who are nothing think they are something, they deceive themselves. (Gal 6:1–2)

I concluded by suggesting that after doing the hard work of soul repair and moral repair, the judge might be eligible (requalified) for some form of public service.

I expected some push back from more conservative viewers who might resist me, an outsider, offering suggestions about how Alabama Christians should relate to one of their leaders. Instead, most of the resistance I received came from more liberal voices, including a couple of my fellow panelists. They seemed to repudiate the notion of grace and redemption and the possibility of a fallen leader serving in the future. But ultimately, I believe in redemption. I have seen it work in the lives of some of the great biblical leaders. One thinks of Moses, David, Peter, and Paul, who seemed to be disqualified from service but experienced redemption and new possibilities. We have seen this in politicians and clergy. And I have experienced redemption and new possibilities in my own life. Note that most of those whom we read about, and who were eligible to lead in the first place, were men. So we must ask whether redemption is and will be available for women who have experienced failures and disappointments. Or is redemption a male phenomenon? To be clear, the gift of redemption should and must be applied to all on an equal basis. Humans are capable of great self-deception. The human mind has mystifying powers of compartmentalization so that one part of the self denies the reality of another part or pretends not to be connected. This is a complex psychological phenomenon and exists along a spectrum of healthy and normal (meaning we are all capable of some of this) and severe psychopathology.

Leaders must hold themselves accountable and seek accountability from trusted others to seek help for severe emotional challenges. We all want leaders to be healthy. It is important that leaders not be hypocrites who proclaim one message while practicing behavior that is diametrically opposed. Hypocrites are aware of the discrepancy between their words and deeds. In the extraordinary play *Tartuffe,* written in 1664, Moliere elaborates on the deceptive exploits of a religious leader named Tartuffe. The story was so powerful and penetratingly honest that the archbishop protested its public performance and urged King Louis XIV to ban it.

It is also important that leaders who are unwell receive the professional intervention they need because, as the popular saying reminds us, "Hurt people, hurt people." And because of their disproportionate influence, visibility, and power, disturbed leaders can inflict immeasurable harm on innocent people.

When it comes to remaining undaunted in the face of failure, I always think about the extraordinary example of former Morehouse president Benjamin E. Mays as he delivered his final commencement address in 1967. In our time, most people do not know the names of many or any college presidents unless there has been a scandal that places that individual into the diet of daily news. But during the 1960s, Benjamin Elijah Mays was known by many who had no connection to the Atlanta University Center. In addition to his popularity as a public speaker and preacher at colleges and universities across America and at the World Council of Churches,

Mays was an adviser to President Lyndon B. Johnson. He was an extraordinary mentor for an entire generation of young people, black and white, who helped to lead the civil rights movement. King referred to Mays as a spiritual mentor who showed him what kind of minister he could become. Mays delivered the benediction at the 1963 March on Washington, at which King delivered the "I Have a Dream" speech. And five days after King's assassination, Mays came out of retirement to deliver the eulogy to a public audience of tens of thousands of people on the Morehouse campus.

Despite all of his stature and achievements, during the final speech as the college president he said something remarkable. The speech was titled, "Twenty Seven Years of Success and Failure at Morehouse." The mere inclusion of the word *failure* in his speech must have disturbed the equilibrium of his audience. Commencements are times for taking bows of self-congratulations. And, for black colleges, commencements acknowledge and celebrate the nexus between the culture of higher education and the culture of the church. People dress as if going to church, and many proud mothers and grandmothers wear their church hats or "crowns." The graduation of a young man, particularly in communities where young black male achievement is infrequent, is a very big deal. In addition, to further charge the environment emotionally, it was the 100th anniversary of the college and the final ceremony for a beloved president of twenty-seven years. No one wanted or expected to hear about failure.

Only Mays knew what he carried in his heart and the sense of disappointment and self-doubt that haunt unique moments and jobs like this. He said:

> I have no regrets in retiring from the presidency of Morehouse at this juncture in history. I regret, however, that what has been accomplished in these twenty-seven years trails so far behind my dreams for the college and so far behind what I aspired for Morehouse to be that I feel a sense of failure. I

wish I could tell you today that the future of Morehouse was guaranteed in the stars. . . . Friends, alumni, trustees, faculty, and students—all share in the success of the college. Likewise, we all share in the college's failure.[61]

Needless to say, few college presidents today speak about their shortcomings. In fact, most of them over promise and under deliver. But Mays reminds us that it is possible to work hard, accomplish much in a career and still feel unfulfilled relative to the dreams and expectations one had for oneself. I can certainly identify with him and am grateful for his example.

A more contemporary example comes from the business sector. In March 2015, Howard Shultz, CEO of Starbucks, launched an initiative aimed at encouraging customers to have safe conversations about race and difference. Race Together, aimed at stimulating conversations about race. Unfortunately, mistakes were made, and the initiative did not go far or persist long. Starbucks concluded the initiative. The online magazine *Eater* reported:

Schultz himself acknowledges one of the biggest flaws in his initiative—people "might find it hard to understand" where his empathy comes from. "I'm not black, I haven't lived a life in which I was racially profiled, and I wasn't discriminated against because of the color of my skin," notes Schultz. Additionally, Starbucks did not spend time "discussing how it would look for a white billionaire to front a national dialogue on race." Instead the company put their effort into scaling up what had worked—the "partner" (employee) forums.[62]

---

[61] Freddie C. Colston, ed., *Benjamin E. Mays Speaks: Representative Speeches of a Great America Orator* (Lanham, MD: University Press of America, 2002), 166.

[62] Khushbu Shah, "Why Starbucks' Race Together Campaign Failed," *Eater* (online magazine) (June 18, 2015).

Starbucks tried something promising and important but failed. Shultz admitted, "Even though when it launched, Race Together seemed to back fire . . . the irony is, we did create a national conversation—not how we intended, but you learn from mistakes."[63] Dr. Mays and Howard Shultz illustrate, variously, that acknowledging institutional mistakes is painful but is a strong demonstration of integrity, courage and imagination. We all can learn from mistakes. This is an essential virtue of effective leadership.

Moral Leaders Invest in the Next Generation by Building Enduring Institutions

Finally, during the course of their lives, moral leaders recognize, as we have said, that they are mortal and must prepare for their eventual transition. Erikson offers wisdom about people who reach the stage and the consciousness of what he calls *generativity,* a state in which the highest motivation of life is investing in the next generation. One does this in a variety of ways at the private level. But at a public level, one cares for all children by building and supporting institutions that will endure far beyond one's life. Dolores Huerta and Cesar Chavez invested in the United Farm Workers, as Ella Baker and Martin Luther King Jr. invested in SCLC. Consequently, the organizations they built extended beyond their lifetimes and sustained their missions well into the future. But another word about Ella Baker that distinguishes her from these other leaders. As biographer Barbara Ransby notes:

> Ella Baker played a pivotal role in the three most prominent black freedom organizations of her day: the National Association for the Advancement of Colored People (NAACP); the Southern Christian Leadership Conference (SCLC); and the Student Nonviolent Coordinating Committee (SNCC).

---

[63] Ibid.

She worked alongside some of the most prominent black male leaders of the twentieth century: W.E.B. Du Bois, Thurgood Marshall, George Schuyler, Walter White, Philip Randolph, Martin Luther King, Jr. and Stokely Carmichael.[64]

But her legacy is special not simply because of her presence and investment in three different organizations. Rather, it was her way of being present that was both disruptive and transformative. Ransby continues:

However, Baker had contentious relationships with all these men and the organizations they headed, with the exception of SNCC during its first six years. For much of her career she functioned as an "outsider within." Baker criticized unchecked egos, objected to undemocratic structures, protested unilateral decision making, condemned elitism, and refused to nod in loyal deference to everything "the leader" had to say. These stances put her on the outside of the inner circle.[65]

I leave further discussion of enduring institutions for the next chapter as we consider the impact of moral leaders. Ultimately, the institutions they establish, support, and invest in represent a key way in which they serve the common good far beyond the limit of their personal lives. Esteemed individuals' lives can be extended and deepened through the mission of a worthy institution.

Moral Leaders Aim to Live Well and Die Well

The fifth dimension of the exemplary life of the moral leader that I wish to highlight is the dignity and humanity of their final

---

[64] Barbara Ransby, *Ella Baker and the Black Freedom Movement: A Radical Democratic Vision* (Chapel Hill: The University of North Carolina Press, 2003), 3.
[65] Ibid., 3–4.

disposition—another way of saying that they die well. Timothy Jackson reminds us that

> a key cornerstone of human solidarity is that we have not created ourselves and that we are all mortal. Some of our greatest moral leaders—Socrates, Jesus, Lincoln, Gandhi, Viola Gregg Liuzzo, the Detroit homemaker who went to Selma and was killed helping Civil Rights volunteers, and Rev. Sharonda Coleman-Singleton, a pastor at Emmanuel AME Church who was among the nine martyrs shot there. They all show us how to die courageously and meaningfully.[66]

As noted earlier, standing for principles that run against the grain of an unjust society puts moral agents and leaders in sharp tension with those who rule and control public instruments of power.

We have looked at the lives of several figures who qualify as moral leaders. I have been impressed by how Niebuhr, King, Baker, Huerta, and Chavez lived into moral agency and moral leadership by becoming students of the moral life who taught through their words and deeds, who framed issues as moral concerns while inviting others to join them, who sought to live exemplary lives but were undaunted in the face of failure. They devoted part of their life to building enduring institutions that extended their impact and legacy as they faced the end of life with dignity, purpose, and contentment.

With all of his faults and maddening contradictions, King's words on the night before he was assassinated still move us and haunt us. What manner of human was this?

> Like anybody, I would like to live a long life—longevity has its place. But I'm not concerned about that now. I just want to do God's will. And He's allowed me to go up to the mountain. And I've looked over, and I've seen the Promised

---

[66] Timothy C. Jackson, email conversation, February 3, 2019.

Land. I may not get there with you, but I want you to know tonight, that we, as a people, will get to the Promised Land. And so I'm happy tonight; I'm not worried about anything; I'm not fearing any man. Mine eyes have seen the glory of the coming of the Lord.[67]

King showed us what to do when incarcerated unjustly, and he demonstrated how to live every day up to the unanticipated last moment with faith and hope, surrounded by friends, preparing for food and fellowship and for the great struggle ahead against violence, racism, and poverty.

---

[67] Martin Luther King Jr., "I've Been to the Mountaintop," address, Bishop Charles Mason Temple, Memphis, Tennessee, April 3, 1968.

3

The Moral Impact of Enduring Institutions

Unnerved by fundamental economic changes and the failure of government to provide lasting solutions, society is increasingly looking to companies, both public and private, to address pressing social and economic issues. . . . (This) must begin with a clear embodiment of your company's purpose in your business model and corporate strategy. . . . Stakeholders are pushing companies to wade into sensitive social and political issues—especially as they see governments failing to do so effectively. As CEOs, we don't always get it right. And what is appropriate for one company may not be for another. . . . One thing, however, is certain: the world needs your leadership.

LARRY FINK,
"PURPOSE AND PROFIT: 2019 LETTER TO CEOS"

I am not merely satisfied in making money for myself, for I am endeavoring to provide employment for hundreds of women of my race.

—MADAM C. J. WALKER

In 1963, an American public moralist wrote a letter to eight clergy leaders in Alabama. The earth moved, slightly. That letter, as we have seen, became a classic of moral argument and political vision. Although addressed to the church, it spoke far beyond the sacred boundaries of a sanctuary. It spoke to the very identity and values of the nation. The letter did exactly what is needed from a public intellectual or, some would say, a prophet. It warned of threats to the nation and offered vision for national renewal. Decades later another leader, this time a business leader, wrote a letter warning of threats to our national economic and social life and our most cherished values. This letter, too, was controversial, earth shaking, and hopeful. The letter was written by Larry Fink, chairman and CEO of BlackRock, the world's largest money manager. The letter offers an ethical and operational invitation to corporate leaders who exercise disproportionate influence in modern society. He offers wisdom about how to lead enduring institutions. And, as is often the case with public intellectuals and prophets, Fink's letter stirred a storm of controversy that continues to reverberate.

In Chapter 1 I set forth a definition of moral leaders as people who live and lead with integrity, courage, and imagination as they serve the common good while inviting others to join them. I invited you to think about those three virtues and about the common good. Then I urged readers to imagine their own "Mount Rushmore" of moral leadership—four leaders, each from a different sector, who are advancing the common good and extending invitations and calls to action. In Chapter 2 I maintained that moral leaders are students of the good and the right, and that they seek to understand and implement what they know about the moral life and the just society. They act to frame issues as moral issues, strive to live exemplary lives and engage in meaningful exemplary action but are not daunted by failure, and build enduring institutions that will outlive them but sustain their values and work. In the end, such leaders also show us how to die, how to approach the end of life with equanimity and openness to what may follow.

We come now to consider the difference moral leaders make. In addition to discussing the nature of enduring and impactful institutions, I offer some criteria and suggestions for making these evaluative judgments. They will take the form of a proposal for principles-centered impact evaluation.

Moral leadership is about more than the moral glamour of solo performances. Sometimes such leaders have to govern, to manage and to exercise keen stewardship over the resources that can facilitate the empowerment of the least advantaged members of society. I hope that some of these observations prove helpful to those who lead organizations, those who govern, and those who are employed or are volunteers of institutions that are seeking to make positive impacts.

My own practical thinking is informed by years of experience providing leadership in several enduring institutions including the Ford Foundation, the Interdenominational Theological Center, Morehouse College in Atlanta, and the Chautauqua Institution in Chautauqua, New York. In addition, I have served on governing and advisory boards for the Salvation Army, the Atlanta Falcons organization, the Joint Center for Political and Economic Studies, and the New York–based think tank, Demos. I highlight here two of these institutions, Chautauqua and Morehouse. Each of them is an American icon, and each has served as a platform for thought leaders and as an incubator for cultivating moral agents and leaders.

Morehouse College, where I was privileged to serve as president, is one of America's leading colleges for producing leaders who have helped change the nation and make history. I arrived at Morehouse aware of the tradition but also anxious to add value. It was an opportunity to invite a couple thousand young men to live lives of success and significance. I was also honored to serve as director of the religion program at the historic Chautauqua Institution, one of the nation's oldest mass gatherings for the arts, ideas, and spirituality. Both institutions can be viewed as case studies to help readers think about the institutions that are part of our lives.

constituted a moral imperative. In contrast, an action done in the hopes of achieving some desired result was hypothetically imperative, meaning that its value depended on determining that the desired result was attained by the hypothesized action. Kant's hypothetical imperatives constitute effectiveness principles. His categorical imperatives are moral principles. Moral principles tell us what is right. Effectiveness principles tell us what works. "Do unto others as you would have them do unto you" provides moral guidance. "Think globally, act locally" offers guidance about how to be effective. Both can be evaluated. Moral principles are evaluated on whether they are being followed, that is, whether you are behaving rightly. Effectiveness principles are evaluated on whether they are being followed and whether, in following them, you achieve what you want to achieve. In that regard, effectiveness principles can be evaluated for their meaningfulness, feasibility, adherence, utility, and results.[5]

Patton offers a valuable paradigm for evaluating the impact of moral leaders. This helps us to ask, did this leader adhere to his or her deeply held moral values? But, also, did the leader achieve the goals of social improvement for others? For communities and a public that respects the nobility of moral values, of serving others, of sacrificing, of struggling, and even of performing extraordinary acts that are not and cannot be obligatory, leaders motivated by what ethicists refer to as *ethical egoism* are regarded to be unprincipled.

In fact, such leaders do have principles, or certainly one principle. They are motivated by the principle of ethical egoism and a transactional logic that asks questions such as the following: Did my activity pay off sufficiently for me? Did I increase my name recognition and expand my network and rolodex? Did I come out first when compared with my peer competitors? Did I sell products and get paid adequately for my services?

---

[5] Ibid., 5.

Conventional morality inquires into whether such a leader has moved the needle of history closer to truth, goodness, righteousness, and beauty. Have lives been improved? Have injustices been redressed? Have laws and policies changed? Has the culture changed? Have leaders and organizations and social movements done the right thing and for the right reasons?

I suggest that moral agents and leaders are concerned with both moral principles and effectiveness; both of these concerns are part of their mode of operating, self-monitoring, and self-evaluating. I also suggest that moral leaders can advance the common good by building and investing in enduring institutions.

Integrity, Courage, and Imagination in the Private Sector

The annual letter by Larry Fink, chairman and CEO of BlackRock, is addressed to fellow CEOs, leaders who set the tone and the agenda for their companies. He stands alongside them, but he also flies at a higher altitude in offering management advice informed by his scan of the larger set of companies they manage and by experts who monitor megatrends.

I noticed that when he offered advice in earlier letters about how to maximize profits and improve performance, there was no controversy. But when in his 2019 letter he suggested that these companies do more to improve the common good and to change their internal cultures, operations, and personnel, the response was strong and direct.

Fink writes: "Society is increasingly looking to companies, both public and private, to address pressing social and economic issues. These issues range from protecting the environment to retirement to gender and racial inequality, among others."[6]

---

[6] Larry Fink, quoted in Charles Gasparino and Lydia Moynihan, "BlackRock's Larry Fink Rattles Employees amid Political Posturing," FoxBusiness online, January 25, 2019.

How does a letter from a public thought leader change the conversation in a substantial way? Following his 2019 letter, in which he called for increased diversity and inclusion, *Forbes* reported that some respondents wrote an article suggesting that Fink was promoting corporate socialism and alleged that BlackRock would lose "the business of major investors who don't agree with Fink's political views."[7]

In a FoxBusiness article Charles Gasparino and Lydia Moynihan reported on reactions to his letter but also to "private remarks to all of BlackRock's employees a day earlier." Fink

> warned managers that their bonuses and pay will decline if they fail to meet diversity hiring targets, while using language to describe the new diversity effort that some BlackRock executives considered offensive. "My leadership team is being measured and their pay is being reflected on how they are driving diversity in their business." BlackRock, he said, is now "putting the pieces in place so that five years from now we'll have a more diverse (company) not just a bunch of white men."[8]

Charles Elson, a corporate governance expert at the University of Delaware, observed, "This is fundamentally not the role of a public company and it's unfair to investors who may not agree with his politics. A CEO shouldn't use house money to further a goal that may not create economic returns."[9]

Fink's courageous and imaginative language and action also upset the equilibrium of some of his own employees. "One BlackRock executive who spoke on the condition of anonymity said, 'This isn't about diversity, it's about identity politics and

---

[7] David Hessekiel, "Has Larry Fink Gone Too Far with Corporate Purpose or Not Far Enough?" *Forbes Magazine* online, January 28, 2019.

[8] Gasparino and Moynihan, "BlackRock's Larry Fink Rattles Employees amid Political Posturing."

[9] Ibid.

virtue signaling that a CEO of a public company shouldn't be engaged in.'"[10]

But challenging narrow interpretations of a company's mandate and the public good, Dale E. Jones, president and CEO of Diversified Search, one of the nation's leading executive-search firms, observes: "Businesses and corporations are ultimately stewards of the public trust. It's not just about shareholder values and returns. Leaders must see the higher calling of their work to promote the greater good of the communities they serve. Hence, the ROI [return on investment] should also reflect the values of inclusion, justice and equity. We have forgotten that the billions of dollars from pension funds (which invest in major corporations) come from blue collar workers, from teachers, firemen, government employees and many others."[11]

The position expressed by Jones is also evident in Walker's quotation at the beginning of this chapter. Sarah Breedlove, known as Madam C. J. Walker, was born in 1867, two years after the end of the Civil War, on a Louisiana plantation. Married at fourteen, she moved with her husband to St. Louis, and became involved in the institutional life of the community attending the St. Paul A.M.E. Church and was active in the National Association of Colored Women. She suffered from scalp ailments and began to explore treatments for herself, which she then marketed to other women. Moving to Denver, she married her third husband, Charles Joseph Walker, and changed her name to Madam C. J. Walker. She hired women to demonstrate and sell scalp treatments in churches, lodges, and clubs throughout the South. She moved to Pittsburgh and opened a school to train others. By 1910, she had settled in Indianapolis, where she built a factory, hair and manicure salon, and another training school. After traveling to Central America and

---

[10] Ibid.

[11] Dale Jones, email to the author, June 9, 2019. Jones is a principles-centered business leader who has helped to engineer and lead change in a variety of America's institutions. I am grateful to him for introducing me to the annual letters of Larry Fink.

the Caribbean to expand her business, in 1916—a year after the death of Booker T. Washington, America's most influential black leader—she moved into a fabulous estate in Harlem and continued to establish habits and standards for corporate and community giving that were informed by her religious faith and commitment to empowering others. She died May 25, 1919.

This view of business as a public trust is also evident in the bold community-serving initiatives being undertaken by Kaiser Permanente chairman and CEO Bernard Tyson. Kaiser is a healthcare consortium based in Oakland, California. As the company sought to make strategic investments to transform the community, Tyson noted: "As we began to prioritize how we were going to focus our community health agenda, this [affordable housing] clearly was one of the critical areas that surfaced to the top floor."[12] Kaiser has invested over $200 million of its impact investment fund to tackle the housing crisis and to offer a model for other cities.[13]

On June 13, 2015, four years before Fink's most controversial letter, civil rights leader, attorney, and banker Vernon Jordan spoke to the baccalaureate ceremony at Stanford University. I was in the audience for my son's graduation. Jordan's title was, "Whom Shall I Send?" He used the occasion to raise ethical concerns about diversity and inclusion there in the heart of Silicon Valley:

> At the beginning of the 20th century, W.E.B. Du Bois, the preeminent Black scholar of his generation, looked at America and declared that "the problem of the twentieth century is the problem of the color-line." Fifteen years into the 21st century I say the problem of America in the 21st century remains the problem of the color line. Yes, that color line faded when Barack Obama raised his right hand on the steps of the Capitol. But, the color line sharpens when Jim Crow is reborn, not

---

[12] Hannah Norman, "Why Housing Is Now a Health Issue for Kaiser Permanente," *San Francisco Business Chronicle* (April 10, 2019).

[13] Ibid.

just in the South, but across America, as a surge of new voter identification laws are enacted by the states. The color line fades when we see black and female CEOs managing America's top companies. And it saddens me to say that here, in this valley of silicon and success, the color line has gone online. The color line persists when black and Latino workers make up just 3 to 4 percent of Silicon Valley's technology workforce but comprise 41 percent of Silicon Valley's security guards, 72 percent of its janitorial staff, and 76 percent of its groundskeepers. . . . The solution is the tough task of getting people registered and out to vote and informed on the issues. It is the slow but necessary process of changing corporate cultures, so that a brother can be a "brogrammer," and a "brogrammer" can be a "sistergrammer." It is the daunting project of shaping institutions that live up to our ideals and ensuring that the winds of freedom truly continue to blow. That is the ultimate test. And that responsibility does not rest on anybody but ourselves. I come today to ask you to join this great struggle.

I come today to ask, as did Isaiah: "Who will go, and whom shall we send?" and I pray that your answer is: "Here am I. Send me."[14]

Following his speech, or sermon, the mood was transformed. This class of graduates, and all young people, had been called—invited—to action for the common good. Their ovation and excitement affirmed the power of an eloquent exemplar who invites others to join in a consequential undertaking.

Moral Leaders Build and Invest in Enduring Institutions

Speaking of evaluating effectiveness, a group of organizational experts produced a fascinating report titled "The World's Most

---

[14] Vernon E. Jordan, Jr., "Whom Shall I Send?" Baccalaureate address, Stanford University, June 13, 2015.

Enduring Institutions." The online magazine *Business Wire* summarized by asking why some institutions endure for decades or even for centuries while others disappear into history. This question sets in motion a business logic and method for determining longevity and performance according to critical business indicators. But some organizational experts recognize that an alternative approach yields a different set of questions and metrics.

In his best-selling and paradigm-shifting book *Good to Great*, Jim Collins identifies several companies that became great by virtue of an ensemble of practices and virtues that were activated and manifest during "inflection points."[15] Reminiscent of Plutarch's method in the first century, Collins develops an inventory of paired companies. But unlike Plutarch, Collins does this to contrast the winners in the market from other companies that faced the challenges and threats of inflection points but failed to make the leap. He highlights the difference between the former group, "great companies," and the latter, "comparator companies" that operate in the same industry as the great ones.

Collins outlines five levels of leadership approaches thus:

- *Level 5: Executive:* Builds enduring greatness through a paradoxical blend of personal humility and professional will.
- *Level 4: Effective Leader:* Catalyzes commitment to and vigorous pursuit of a clear and compelling vision, stimulating higher performance standards.
- *Level 3: Competent Manager:* Organizes people and resources toward the effective and efficient pursuit of predetermined objectives.
- *Level 2: Contributing Team Member:* Contributes individual capabilities to the achievement of group objectives and works effectively with others in a group setting.

---

[15] Jim Collins, *Good to Great: Why Some Companies Make the Leap . . . and Other Don't* (New York: William Collins, 2001).

- *Level 1: Highly Capable Individual:* Makes productive contributions through talent, knowledge, skills, and good work habits.[16]

This hierarchy shows the need for more moral leadership in the business sector. But it is also a reminder to nonprofit leaders to blend the effective stewardship that business disciplines can inform along with their mission values to serve the common good.

Booz Allen Hamilton, the global strategy and technology consulting firm, sponsored a project that identified ten of the world's most enduring institutions over the past century. "The list celebrates those institutions that have managed to reinvent themselves time and again—and remained market leaders—as the unique circumstances of their founding have given way to changing conditions."[17] The criteria employed to identify exemplary institutions were interesting.

Each institution is recognized for its unique abilities to meet or exceed seven specific criteria for an Enduring Institution:

1. Innovative capabilities—The capacity to create and modify strategies based on market opportunities and threats.
2. Governance and leadership—A leadership structure and senior management team that promote an organization-wide commitment to enterprise resilience.
3. Information flow—A continual flow of information regarding an organization's operations and markets that is evaluated by senior management in making strategic decisions.
4. Culture and values—A working environment in which the adaptive qualities required for enterprise resilience are cultivated.

---

[16] Ibid., 20.

[17] "Booz Allen Hamilton Lists the World's Most Enduring Institutions; Joins with Leading Scholars to Identify Ten Institutions That Have Adapted, Endured and Prevailed," Business Wire website, December 16, 2004. Business Wire provides a helpful summary of the contents of the original report.

5. Adaptive response—The ability to withstand operational disruptions, market risks and other threats without significantly compromising an organization's effectiveness.

6. Risk structure—A system for managing risk that doesn't encumber or limit an organization's operations.

7. Legitimacy—The undisputed, withstanding credibility of an organization within its market.[18]

These criteria are somewhat abstract, but they become more comprehensible when we look at the ten organizations that the panel of scholars and experts identified as exemplary of the various qualities: General Electric, Rockefeller Foundation, the American Constitution, the International Telecommunication Union, the Salvation Army, the modern Olympic games, Dartmouth College, Oxford University, Sony, and, somewhat amusingly, the Rolling Stones, a rock band that has evolved each decade to appeal to a changing fan base.

I find Collins's analysis quite compelling and more helpful than the original Booz Allen Hamilton report. Following the success of his 2001 book, Collins noticed that more and more nonprofit organizations—universities, churches, and community organizations, for example—were facing pressure to operate like for-profit businesses, conforming to the same logic and disciplines of the business world. Sitting in the board meetings of numerous nonprofit organizations whose memberships are increasingly populated, if not dominated, by business leaders, it is certainly the case that business logic may be replacing the "mission logic" of the organization. Collins highlights key differences between the business and social sectors.

The confusion between inputs and outputs stems from one of the primary differences between business and the social sectors. In business, money is both an input (a resource for achieving greatness) *and* an output (a measure of greatness). In

---

[18] Ibid.

the social sectors, money is only an input, and not a measure of greatness.[19]

Collins then offers a key insight that should help us all to be more conscious of which logic and metrics are in the driver's seat.

A great organization is one that delivers superior performance and makes a distinctive impact over a long period of time. For a business, financial returns are a perfectly legitimate measure of performance. For a social sector organization, however, performance must be assessed relative to mission, not financial returns. In the social sectors, the critical question is not "How much money do we make per dollar of invested capital?" but "How effectively do we deliver on our mission and make a distinctive impact, relative to our resources?"[20]

I know firsthand that difficult conversations occurred in many college and university board meetings during the height of the Great Recession as scores of students and their families were forced abruptly to discontinue their college educations. Courageous board and institutional leaders acknowledged that although there were limits to how much small liberal-arts colleges with modest endowments could subsidize first-generation low-income students, their mission required them to do more for their students than other schools and external credit-rating agencies considered prudent. In the end, thousands of students were able to continue their educations even while the schools absorbed the double hit of having their credit ratings downgraded and their revenues severely depleted, a regrettable case of good deeds being punished.

I was present, however, on a fateful morning at the Morehouse College commencement when a billionaire philanthropist made

[19] Jim Collins, *Good to Great and the Social Sectors: A Monograph to Accompany Good to Great* (New York: HarperCollins, 2005), 5.
[20] Ibid.

a transformative gift to pay off the entire student debt of nearly four hundred graduating seniors. Robert F. Smith had delivered a thoughtful and autobiographical speech highlighting key practices and principles that led to his success, such as, "There is no substitute for doing the work." As he approached the end of his speech, he said that he was going to put a little "fuel in the tank" of this class. Anticipation grew for those who were still listening. Then he announced that on behalf of the eight generations of his family that inhabited America, his family was making a grant to eliminate their entire student debt. There was a slight pause in the crescendo of ecstatic response and then the students, and many parents, erupted in joy. It was a wonderful affirmation of the importance of investing in enduring institutions.

Enduring institutions have strong cultures that enable them to invite deep participation and evoke deep loyalty. Ultimately, they are good organizations if they serve social ends. In the corporate arena, corporate social responsibility represents this aspiration to do good for humanity and not simply for the financial bottom line.

Increasingly, social entrepreneurs and ethicists are insisting that companies and leaders consider at least a triple bottom line, that is, impacts on *people, planet,* and *profits.* An old conversation about the corrosive effects of unbridled global capitalism going back to Adam Smith in his *Theory of Moral Sentiments* is being refreshed and extended in important ways, particularly in the application of moral theory to the political economy. Notable are edited works by Ted A. Smith and Robert P. Jones, and deliberations under way in Europe by Christoph Lutge and Christoph Strosetzki, among others.[21] (This is the conversation Dr. King was pursuing in his final days.[22])

---

[21] Ted A. Smith and Robert P. Jones, eds., *Spirit and Capital in an Age of Inequality* (Abingdon, TN: Routledge Press, 2017); see also, Christoph Lutge and Christoph Strosetzki, eds., *The Honorable Merchant: Between Modesty and Risk Taking: Intercultural and Literary Aspects* (Munich: Technical University of Munich, 2019).

[22] Cornel West, Tavis Smiley, Clayborn Carson, and others have insisted that greater attention be given to King's class analysis through the length of his public ministry.

In order to endure, institutions must observe certain disciplines and function effectively. But they must also operate in accord with their mission. As Collins notes: "It doesn't really matter whether you can quantify your results. What matters is that you rigorously assemble evidence—quantitative or qualitative—to track your progress."[23] Ultimately, Collins and others urge all organizational leaders to practice a discipline of leadership, management, and assessment that is disciplined and moral.

Building on the insights of the report entitled "World's Most Enduring Institutions" is a text that I have found valuable in evaluating the health of all organizations. Leaders would be prudent to focus on the processes and questions that can help them to better understand and renew the vitality of their organizations. The book is *Beyond Performance: How Great Organizations Build Ultimate Competitive Advantage* by Scott Keller and Colin Price.[24] It has been characterized as a manifesto for a new way of thinking about organizations. My firsthand experience with it occurred at Emory University, which used the approach to build its strategic plan under a dynamic new president.

Keller and Price suggest that "focusing on organizational health—the ability of your organization to align, execute, and renew itself faster than your competitors can—is just as important as focusing on the traditional drivers of business performance."[25] Over time and in dialogue with numerous managers and leaders from various sectors, they evolved a set of diagnostic categories and questions that can focus leaders on key dimensions of organizational health. These "five frames" are *aspire, assess, architect, act,* and *advance.*[26] I summarize these briefly in order to encourage institutional leaders and boards

---

[23] Collins, *Good to Great and the Social Sectors: A Monograph to Accompany Good to Great,* 7.

[24] Scott Keller and Colin Price, *Beyond Performance: How Great Organizations Build Ultimate Competitive Advantage* (Hoboken, NJ: John Wiley and Sons, 2011).

[25] Ibid., xiv.

[26] Ibid., 20.

who govern them to think through each category as they consider their strategic direction and contributions to the public good.

1. *Aspire:* Where do we want to go? How to develop a change vision and targets (the strategic objectives). How to determine what "healthy" looks like for an organization (the health essentials).
2. *Assess:* How ready are we to go there? How to identify and diagnose an organization's ability to achieve its vision and targets (the capability platform). How to uncover the root-cause mindsets that drive organizational health (the discovery process).
3. *Architect:* What do we need to do to get there? How to develop a concrete, balanced set of initiatives to improve performance (the portfolio of initiatives). How to reshape the work environment to influence healthy mindsets (the influence model).
4. *Act:* How do we manage the journey? How to determine and execute the right scaling-up approach for each initiative in the portfolio (the delivery model). How to ensure that energy for change is continually infused and unleashed (the change engine).
5. *Advance:* How do we keep moving forward? How to make the transition from a transformation focused on a one-time step change to an era of ongoing improvement efforts (the continuous improvement infrastructure). How to lead transformation and sustain high performance from a core of self-mastery (centered leadership).[27]

Again, the value of the model comes from paying attention both to *performance* and to *institutional health,* not one or the other. All of us have old mobile phones, laptops and other devices that

---

[27] Ibid.

performed well when we first acquired them. But the companies that produced them were not very healthy and they did not endure. Leaders must think about both sides of the equation.

Perhaps more interesting than their argument for managing and leading an organization dynamically so that it can "both shape its environment and rapidly adapt to it"[28] is their observation about the changing role of the workplace in our time:

> The role of business in society is changing. As we work more and socialize less, the time we have left for traditional activities involving our family, our local community, and our religious institutions is declining. As a result, our sense of meaning and identity is increasingly derived from the workplace (our jobs) and the marketplace (the products and services we buy).[29]

The transformation of the workplace into a zone of social meaning and identity, an extension of our selves, helps us to apprehend the assumptions underlying Larry Fink's annual letters to CEOs.

I turn now to sharing reflections on two enduring institutions with strong cultures, the kinds of cultures that transform them into incubators for confident moral agents and moral leaders.

Chautauqua Institution:
Arts, Knowledge, Spirituality, and Wholesome Leisure

The Chautauqua Institution is an iconic American institution founded in 1874, yet most Americans know little about it. As one who lived, worked, and led there, I know that it is one of the most remarkable places in the country. By highlighting it here, I hope that the curiosity of more people will be stimulated to learn more and someday pay a visit during the nine-week summer season

---

[28] Ibid., xvi.
[29] Ibid.

featuring the arts, great ideas, diverse spirituality, and wholesome leisure.

During the summer Chautauqua County in western New York, near Erie, Pennsylvania, is a rich green bouquet of natural beauty and history. As an aside, I note that during winter months another side of its beauty is revealed and framed in frost and snow. My first official day on the job was in January 2014, when a fierce wind met and taunted me to consider the futility of human existence. But summer is the reward for all who endure the punishing cruelty of winter.

Chautauqua Institution was a nineteenth-century answer to the modern question of how Americans would spend their leisure time as the blessings and burdens of modern industrial life engulfed them. Following the Civil War, the nation was engaged, as Abraham Lincoln put it, in binding wounds. Many perceived that a new threat was looming, that is, the industrialization of the economy, with population shifts from rural to urban communities, and new strains upon American marriage and family life. With laborers having more disposable time and income, people worried that men would become less responsible and available to their families, misusing their newly acquired time in drunkenness and other domestic pastimes. *The Vertigo Years: Europe, 1900–1914,* sketches the dramatic changes of that period as they unfolded in Europe, with many parallels to what occurred in America.[30] Of course, all of this was unfolding as the color line in these societies excluded its people of color from equal access to the benefits of modernity.

Chautauqua was one of the institutions that emerged to instruct Americans on the art of wholesome leisure. Founded by a Methodist pastor and a businessman, Chautauqua started as a summer campground gathering but evolved into an elaborate summer program. Its stage served as a pulpit for several US presidents—including Ulysses S. Grant in the first year after its founding, and

---

[30] Philipp Blom, *The Vertigo Years: Europe, 1900–1914* (New York: Basic Books, 2008).

Franklin D. Roosevelt during World War II, when and where he delivered his "I Hate War" speech.

The campus where hundreds of tents were pitched by the lake for lectures, singing, and worship today feels more like a liberal-arts college campus, containing housing from cabins and modest gingerbread houses, to modern condos and multi-million-dollar mansions. Four departments organize the multiplicity of lectures, concerts, worship gatherings, and classes. I led the religion department, which hosted some of the world's most influential public intellectuals and Christian preachers, addressing critical ideas and issues of the day. The lecture platform could be regarded as an "A list" of moral and thought leaders.[31]

Indeed, it is because Chautauqua successfully invited and hosted world-class speakers, artists, and preachers that it has attracted a large multigenerational following. The many distinguished speakers have included Eleanor Roosevelt, Booker T. Washington, opera singer Marian Anderson, cellist Yo Yo Ma, Motown artists like Diana Ross and Smokey Robinson, Johnny Mathis, Nancy Wilson, the Temptations, jazz trumpeter Wynton Marsalis, and, as mentioned above, several US presidents.

Among the speakers hosted by the religion department were individuals whom I believed to be moral leaders. As they spoke, each of them informed and refined my thoughts about this topic and are part of the inspiration for this work. I'll highlight a few that stand out for me.

---

[31] An incredibly talented group of leaders collaborate to plan and host the thousands of programs and activities that occur each year, most during the summer seasons. I worked with two amazing presidents, Tom Becker and Michael Hill, as they huddled with program leaders like Sherra Babcock and Matt Ewalt in the education department. In the religion department I succeeded Rev. Dr. Joan Brown Campbell and was succeeded by Director Maureen Rovegno and Vice President Bishop Gene Robinson, music director Jared Jacobsen (recently deceased), and Hall of Mission hosts Bill and Maggie Brockman. The arts program was guided for many years by Marty Merkely and later by Deborah Sunya Moore.

Sister Simone Campbell is the driving force behind Nuns on the Bus, who visit members of Congress and express their ethical and political concerns. She has focused on the corrosive effects of dramatic disparities in wealth and income. On the afternoon she spoke in the Hall of Philosophy, she illustrated wealth and income inequality in a memorable way. She continues her work of advocacy for economic justice rooted in the moral authority of the 1986 US Catholic Bishops's pastoral letter on Catholic social teaching and the US economy, *Economic Justice for All*.[32]

Marian Wright Edelman, founder of the Children's Defense Fund, electrified Chautauqua by making her case that the well being of children should serve as the moral litmus test of a good and just society. She reminded listeners that the great moral teachers were concerned about the nurture of children. Her organization's mission statement elaborates comprehensive development by prescribing a series of "starts," including a *"Healthy Start,* a *Head Start,* a *Fair Start,* a *Safe Start,* and a *Moral Start* in life and successful passage to adulthood with the help of caring families and communities."

Rev. William Barber developed a national reputation by leading a series of progressive activist vigils—Moral Mondays—in Raleigh, North Carolina. Most people came to know him when he called the nation to consider its "heart condition" and degree of compassion for marginalized people in a stirring address to the July 2016 Democratic National Convention. At Chautauqua, a capacity crowd gathered on a humid afternoon to hear Dr. Barber plead for a new moral reconstruction of national policy and priorities that care for the plight of the least advantaged in a wealthy society.

Rev. Dr. Joan Brown Campbell was general secretary of the National Council of Churches. She helped put a human face on the crisis of refugee families who are separated. After her term as general secretary, Rev. Dr. Campbell became Chautauqua's first female director of religion and senior pastor. During the 1960s she

---

[32] US Catholic Bishops, *Economic Justice for All: Pastoral Letter on Catholic Social Teaching on the US Economy* (Washington, DC: USCCB, 1986).

was an associate of Dr. King and helped coordinate his visits to her hometown of Cleveland. Rev. Dr. Campbell achieved international recognition when she became involved in the Elian Gonzalez immigration and custody dispute in 2000 between Cuba and the United States. She bonded with young Elian's grandmothers and ultimately prepared the way for him to return to Cuba and his extended family. Chautauquans were deeply moved by the tragic story and heroic presence of Dr. Izzeldin Abuelaish, a Palestinian–Canadian physician who lost three of his daughters during tank fire by Israel's military in Gaza. His book, *I Shall Not Hate,* is compelling reading.[33] Abuelaish has been nominated for a Nobel Peace Prize and is known by many as the Gaza Doctor. It was compelling to see him, along with his surviving daughters, dressed in hijabs, enjoy hospitality at the home of a courageous Jewish Chautauquan who is committed to fostering peace, enlightenment, and understanding at the human level.

Rabbi Jonathan H. Sacks, retired chief rabbi of the United Hebrew Congregations of the Commonwealth UK, has challenged a violent world in his book, *Not in God's Name: Confronting Religious Violence.*[34] For many who despair of ever seeing a peaceful resolution to violence in the Middle East, Rabbi Sacks brings a humorous, self-critical, and hopeful approach to finding common ground, speaking truth, and acknowledging the need for generosity of spirit.

One of the most charismatic leaders I observed at Chautauqua is Father Gregory Joseph Boyle, a Jesuit priest and founder of Homeboy Industries in Los Angeles. In 1988, he addressed the unmet needs of gang-involved youth by developing job and entrepreneurial opportunities. His program is regarded as the largest and most successful gang-rehabilitation and reentry program in the world. He came to Chautauqua along with several of the young

---

[33] Izzeldin Abuelaish, *I Shall Not Hate: A Gaza Doctor's Journey on the Road to Peace and Human Dignity* (New York: Bloomsbury, 2012).

[34] Rabbi Jonathan H. Sacks, *Not in God's Name: Confronting Religious Violence* (New York: Random House, 2015).

men who were alumni of Homeboy Industries. These muscle-bound, tattooed young men reminded me of the guys who almost fought in front of my grandmother's house. They were virtual rock stars as they walked around the Chautauqua campus and presented their life stories in various settings.

Boyle, a self-deprecating and humorous urban priest, disarmed audiences as he recounted hopeful and often heartbreaking interactions with the young people in his community. Although scandals were surfacing in the Catholic church during the very week of his visit, he challenged people to focus on the evidence of life-changing ministry and not simply cases of abuse.

Rev. Barbara Skinner, an African American evangelical (and widow of the famed evangelist Tom Skinner) is founder of the National Prayer Breakfast at the Congressional Black Caucus. She joined S. Douglas Birdsall, a white Christian missionary from Peoria, Illinois, on the stage as they spoke candidly about working together to heal the racial divide in the evangelical world. They have convened confidential leadership dialogues that have exposed many prominent white and black leaders to possibilities for understanding, empathy, and reconciliation.

Bill Moyers, television journalist and video documentarian, himself became part of an unexpected drama prior to his presentation. That Monday morning in 2016, the Chautauqua audience expected to hear a young charismatic leader of the Black Lives Matter movement (#BLM), DeRay Mckesson. He was to be the opening keynote speaker, but that weekend he organized a #BLM protest in Baton Rouge against the police killing of Alton Sterling. During the protest a police officer was struck by a rock. Mckesson did not throw the rock or encourage such behavior, but he was charged. Can or should organizers be charged with incitement of violence that they did not endorse? That was among the legal questions that he and his lawyers had to address. He was to be released on the morning that we expected him on our stage. Meanwhile, the Chautauqua planning team went into motion and recognized that Bill Moyers, Ambassador Andrew Young, Reverend Raphael Warnock, and Ouleye Warnock, a doctoral candidate in international politics, were all there for speaking assignments at different times of that week. We invited them to a breakfast planning session and created a panel of all four figures to be moderated by Moyers. It proved to be a transformative conversation as they confronted difficult issues of pursuing racial justice, racial reconciliation, and strategies of social change.

There are many other extraordinary moral leaders who have spoken at Chautauqua. I regret that there is not sufficient space to discuss each one who is deserving.[35] These extraordinary leaders have infused hope into our global community, and much of that wisdom was shared and celebrated at Chautauqua. Each week of the summer, Chautauqua sends thousands of people back to their local communities to infuse them with new knowledge and perspective, a passion for civility and a relentless commitment to progressive, positive change.

At its height, Chautauqua became a movement that swept the nation. *Chautauqua* even became a verb meaning "to gather for an enriching, intellectually stimulating experience." Smaller "daughter Chautauquas" sprang up around the nation, with almost 250 at one point. Today, only thirty or forty survive. But this practice of

---

[35] These moral leaders include Eboo Patel of Interfaith Youth Core; Dr. Tink Tinker, a Native American liberation theologian from Denver; Rev. Raphael Warnock, senior pastor of Ebenezer Baptist Church; Dr. Katharine Rhodes Henderson, president of Auburn Seminary; Rabbi Joseph Telushkin of Brooklyn; Rev. Michael McBride of Oakland; Sister Joan Chittister, a Benedictine nun and theologian; Imam Abdul Malik Mujahid, former chair of the World Parliament of Religions; Dr. Helene Gayle, president of the Chicago Community Trust; Rev. Otis Moss III, senior pastor of Trinity United Church of Christ; Dr. Pamela R. Lightsey, a United Methodist elder and queer lesbian; Lobsang Tenzin Negi, Buddhist director of the Emory-Tibet Science Initiative; and Dr. Mae Jemison, the nation's first African American astronaut.

replicating Chautauqua across the nation is evidence of its inspiring legacy and the long reach of nineteenth-century traditions that deserve to endure.

Chautauqua takes seriously its mission to welcome and engage the best that has been thought, said, and performed, and it seeks to preserve humanistic practices like long conversations on front porches with old friends and new acquaintances. The women's movement was born in Seneca Falls near the grounds in western New York—it was the location of the first national gathering of women to advocate full voting rights for white women—and Chautauqua has been associated with many progressive values and movements for transforming America.

In addition to welcoming influential Americans like Eleanor Roosevelt, Thurgood Marshall, Justice Sandra Day O'Connor, and pilot Amelia Earhart (who landed her plane on the Chautauqua golf course), Chautauqua helped to launch America's oldest ongoing book club (Chautauqua Literary and Scientific Circle) and had a correspondence course that enabled readers to receive new books and come to the campus grounds for a commencement ceremony.[36] There are inspiring stories of how Americans in remote parts of the western United States awaited the mail delivery each month of the Chautauqua book selection.

Chautauqua is now courageously engaged in a process of embracing greater diversity and learning to celebrate race and difference, and to demonstrate generosity and hospitality to the LGBTQ community. President Michael Hill and the board have made diversity and inclusivity core components of the institution's strategic plan. An African American Heritage House has emerged to help advance these goals.

---

[36] For a list of the books recommended by the Chautauqua Literary and Scientific Circle from its founding in 1878 to 2018, see "CLSCBookList.pdf," available online.

Morehouse: A Center of Excellence for Public-Centered Leadership Development

All liberal-arts colleges are remarkable and wonderful places, and Morehouse is especially so. It was founded in 1867 in the ashes of the Civil War. Its benefactor, John D. Rockefeller, founder of Standard Oil and a loyal Baptist layman, donated the land for the campus (along with land for the campus of Spelman College, a school named in honor of his wife). From the beginning, the school became a liberal arts leadership academy. It had a policy of admitting all of the nation's black male high school valedictorians. Howard Thurman was one of those valedictorians.

Dr. John Hope was the college's first black president. Benjamin E. Mays, who first came to Morehouse in 1927 to teach after earning his master's degree at Chicago, assumed the office of president in 1940 and went on to serve for twenty-seven years. Mays helped to recruit and attract the faculty leaders that made the college remarkable. Morehouse earned membership in Phi Beta Kappa thanks to its legendary professors, many of whom taught young Martin Luther King Jr. and the generations of pioneers and public servants who followed him.

The modern civil rights movement would certainly not have been as effective without the extraordinary contributions of the graduates of Morehouse—the Morehouse men. Aside from King, they included Julian Bond, Maynard Jackson, Surgeon General David Hatcher, Secretary of Health and Human Services Louis Sullivan, and some of the nation's most talented pastors, congressmen, business leaders, engineers, college presidents, artists, and community leaders.

Years later I arrived as president of Morehouse and found the culture to be strong but in need of updating and refining for a millennial, high-tech era. As the college grew in size, it began to shed many of its early traditions. After studying the college history and interviewing key alumni, board members, and donors, I pondered how I could build on and extend the institutional building ministry of Benjamin E. Mays and his successors, humanities scholar Hugh M. Gloster, business entrepreneur Leroy Keith, and physicist Walter E. Massey.

I knew that once my appointment as president was announced, the media would ask about my vision and what precisely is a Morehouse man? I was always dissatisfied with vague responses to this question, even by the college, and felt that we could and should be confident, committed, and crisp in articulating our answer. I began a process of crafting a vision that I hoped might bring renewed pride and dedication in the Morehouse family. It came to be known as the Morehouse Renaissance. I spoke of students as Renaissance men with social conscience and global perspective. And I proposed an aspirational vision for every student, namely, that he aspire to the "five wells": becoming well read, well spoken, well traveled, well dressed, and well balanced.

I first delivered a speech outlining the "five wells" in 2008. I had initially begun to hammer out the language during my attendance at the New Presidents' Seminar sponsored by Harvard's Graduate School of Education. I shared the vision with my staff, who raised questions and made suggestions. Finally, it was ready for prime time. The parents in the orientation audience for new students were the first to hear it, and they expressed their appreciation for the articulation of high expectations of personal decorum and dignity. I did not expect the standing ovation that followed. But it reminded me that Morehouse plays a unique role in the psyche of many African American communities.

I will always cherish the day that I walked across campus from the campus barbershop toward my office. There on the sidewalk was the director Spike Lee, holding forth with a large group of students. We brightened to see each other and he thanked me for stopping by. I thanked him for coming to campus regularly to challenge our students intellectually. He smiled and observed that "some of the brothers are talking about how you all are telling them to take off their hats in class." He smiled with a long pause. Recalling the legacy of some of the great Morehouse men—Benjamin Mays, Martin Luther King Jr., and Maynard Jackson—I replied, "Yes, Spike, we are saying that they can wear whatever they please when they are off campus or after hours in the dorms, but when they come to chapel and class, when they meet and are observed by large numbers of visitors, donors, and media, we ask that they look more like Mays, Martin, and Maynard." He seemed to accept that, but I knew that the students were observing how Spike had crafted his own look and public presentation. Addressing the students, I said, "When you achieve success as an independent entrepreneur or artist, you can do what he has done, but until then, it is a good idea to observe the soft cultural norms of leadership."

As I walked away, I reminded myself that such a challenge to moral norms is good and healthy, and that moral agents should have reasons to justify and explain their position. In a moment of serendipity, as I approached Gloster Hall and King Chapel, a woman was waiting to speak to me. She was a parent who had attended the orientation days earlier. She said, "Dr. Franklin, I never expected to hear this, but my son told me we would need to go shopping as he wanted to have dress shirts and slacks. He came here with only three pairs of shorts and T-shirts. I was so happy I almost cried." That was one day in the life of a Morehouse president.

Some argue that the school's expectations are heteronormative and even homophobic. I think the first concern has some validity in privileging traditional norms of dress and decorum. But the norms are not and should not be interpreted to be homophobic. Same-gender-loving men have always been visible and accepted as members of this particular village. That speaks to institutional commitments to inclusivity, respect, and civility. It is unfortunate that these values have not always been observed worthy and embraced by members of this diverse community. In fact, the tensions, disagreements, and arguments that occasionally emerge in all communities, perhaps especially in the remaining male organizations and schools, expose deeper divides in the larger community and society at large. Many institutions, including houses of worship, schools, and other social organizations must continue to work on managing diversity and civility in the community. And it is important for institutions to declare unambiguously that disrespect and violence are immoral, if not criminal, and will not be tolerated.

A Woman's Voice in Men's Space

In August 2015, the *New York Times* published an article titled "Parents' Ceremony Serves Up Elements of Morehouse Gospel."[37] It describes the rituals that compose an elaborate multi-day process of handing over young students to the college that will be home for the coming years.

I have observed and experienced other "parting" occasions on other campuses. Most have been unceremonious, almost amounting to a dropping off, that is, the new freshman arrives and gets settled in as parents and family conclude this phase of the transition. Most schools do not acknowledge or ritualize the powerful emotions that may surround such occasions. Even in my own entry to Morehouse in 1975, my father did not make the trip from Chicago, and my mother said goodbye on the curb as a taxi waited outside Graves Hall, the oldest building on campus where registration occurred.

But by 1996, Morehouse had recognized the missed opportunity of helping parents grapple with separation anxiety and fear of the unknown. More than that, the ceremony also provides a unique framework of meaning and purpose for the young men who can "choose to attend any college in the country."[38] It is an extraordinary ritual developed by talented Morehouse staff, including the college chaplain, associate provost, and others. It includes readings

---

[37] Samuel G. Freedman, "Parents' Ceremony Serves Up Elements of 'Morehouse Gospel,'" *New York Times,* August 21, 2015.

[38] Ibid.

from sacred and cultural texts; African drumming; music and dance; call-and-response statements; depositing handwritten cards of hopes, dreams, and wishes for their sons; and a ritual march out of the chapel into the street where rows of alumni stand to oversee this transfer of human capital.

The narrative and flow of the ritual tap into powerful emotions and myths that nearly everyone present can understand. The ritual leader begins by invoking memories of this incoming freshman as a young boy taking his first steps, stumbling, and then over time mastering the art of walking. It is significant that this leader has been a woman, Dr. Anne Wimberly Watts, a professor of English and a speech coach. A woman's voice in a men's college immediately creates the sense of a village. I have always thought of this as the presence of the sacred feminine co-presiding over a life-changing transition. Over many years of diligent service she has earned a unique honorific from students reserved for only one person, namely, Mother Morehouse.

Dr. Watts is a remarkable college leader who not only has led this ritual but also led change in this all-men's school. She reports that when she arrived in the late 1960s at the request of Dr. Mays, she and other women on campus were often called upon to constitute an informal hospitality committee to "pour tea."[39] She mentored both the young students on campus and the female staff, whom she helped to become protocol facilitators for the many high-profile events that came to campus. She challenged the women at Morehouse, who were often invisible or treated with perfunctory courtesy by the men, to take classes and to improve their own education. She insisted on everyone treating them with dignity and respect. As the daughter of a prominent Baptist pastor in Grambling, Louisiana, she knew a lot about the power of individual moral agency and the power of ritual action in enduring institutions.

---

[39] Interview with Dr. Anne Wimberly Watts, Paschal's Restaurant, Atlanta, Georgia, June 21, 2019.

Back to the parent's parting ceremony. As the ritual unfolds, the audience hears words from Khalil Gibran's poem "On Children." These words prepare the heart for separation with grace and assurance.

> And a woman who held a babe against her bo-
> som said,
> Speak to us of Children. And he said:
> Your children are not your children.
> They are the sons and daughters of Life's longing
> for itself.
> They come through you but not from you,
> And though they are with you yet they belong
> not to you.
> You may give them your love but not your
> thoughts
> For they have their own thoughts.[40]

Then, the ritual leader's voice rises in a slow crescendo,

All of those years, all of that sacrifice, all of those prayers now lead to this moment. The moment when you will give your son up. You must let him go. It is hard to do. Remember when he was learning to ride his bicycle? When you removed the training wheels, you ran alongside him and held the little handle bars to keep him safe. But, then, you realized that you have to let them go in order for him to ride. If you do not let him go, he will not grow, he will not soar, he cannot become the man you want him to be. He cannot become what God wants him to be unless you let him go! You have brought him to this moment. Now, release him and let him go! Let go of the handle bars!

---

[40] Kahlil Gibran, "On Children," *The Prophet* (New York: Alfred Knopf, 1923).

Parents are holding back tears. One can hear sniffles and see glistening eyes throughout the vast hall.

Then, with dramatic power, she proclaims, "Now parents, call his name! And as you shout his name, think of how much you love him. Call his name!" The room vibrates with the shouts of two thousand voices raised. "Call his name! Let the heavens hear that he matters and he is in good hands. Call his name!"

Parents are now openly weeping. There are no dry eyes among the over twenty-five-hundred people gathered. There is pure joy and pure pain in this emotionally rich and charged moment.

Then the young men stand together and walk out of King Chapel bordered by hundreds of alumni outside awaiting them. They march in single file into the gates of the college. The gates are closed after them. The parents stand outside watching and are assured that these gates will not open again for them as a cohort until the day of their graduation.

As I write about this ritual and graduation, I mention again the memorable hot Sunday morning when a class of over 390 graduating seniors heard their commencement speaker, philanthropist Robert F. Smith, declare that he would put "a little fuel in (their) bus by paying off their student loan debt." It was hot, and he had spoken for an extended time when he reached this point in the speech. He had spoken earlier about riding segregated buses across Denver to attend a nice private school. Now, each student would be in the driver's seat of his own bus to help lead the community.

The response to his announcement was electric but delayed. Those who listened closely immediately apprehended what he intended. Many others awaited the echo to sink in. We all wanted an instant replay on the jumbo screens, but soon it sunk in. This class of students would leave college with no debt. Parents, perhaps many of them deeply indebted and on financial thin ice, shouted and cried, again.

His direct challenge to alumni and the college was electrifying: "I challenge you to do more." I hope that his words will become a compelling invitation to all alumni to support their fellow students and to all citizens to invest in the creative people who will improve our communities and nation in the future.

Although Robert F. Smith's gift was the largest financial gift received by the college, it followed the extraordinary philanthropy of Oprah Winfrey years earlier.[41] No one who viewed the final three episodes of Oprah's TV show can forget what occurred on the evening of May 24, 2011. With a capacity crowd in the United Center in Chicago, following a tribute from Gayle King and Maria Kennedy Shriver, a brief introduction from Tyler Perry, and a touching solo by Kristin Chenoweth, hundreds of our students walked into the dark stadium carrying candles, a powerful affirmation that moral leaders do not curse the darkness but light candles. Meanwhile, standing alone on the stage, Oprah wept in gratitude for this stunning visual reminder of the change that her investments enabled.[42] Oprah herself said that is when she went into an "ugly cry" as did all of the Hollywood celebrities who viewed backstage. My wife and I watched in awe from the balcony.

Morehouse men live with the metaphor of a crown held above their heads into which they may grow through service to others. That image emerged from Dr. Howard Thurman, a Christian mystic and dean of Marsh Chapel at Boston University, dean of Rankin Chapel at Howard University, and cofounder of a multiracial and multifaith congregation in San Francisco during the 1940s, just after World War II.

It was in the Morehouse chapel that I first heard and met Thurman. He had a special way with words. He shared the story of growing up as a boy in rural Florida and going to a friend's house to play. When he arrived, the father told him to come in the front

---

[41] Oprah Winfrey has provided over $13 million to over four hundred Morehouse students over the years. See Celia Fernandez, "Oprah Just Responded to an Instragram Commenter Who Insinuated She Doesn't Give Enough Money Back," *The Oprah Magazine* (May 20, 2019).

[42] See "Morehouse Men Thank Oprah Winfrey" on YouTube.

door rather than going to the yard. He found the father, mother, and his friend pressed against the window observing something terrifying and remarkable. The boy's two-year-old sister was sitting on the ground in the backyard with a rattlesnake in her lap. Not wanting to run out and possibly startle the snake, which might bite the girl, they watched, ready to run to the rescue. But they observed something amazing. The girl stroked the snake as it slowly wrapped itself around her body and neck. The snake and the girl were playing with each other. Finally, the girl pulled the snake off and walked into the house as the snake retreated into the woods.

Thurman told us that there were two natural enemies interacting, and slowly they transcended their predicted roles of attacking and frightening the other. He spoke of the possibility of transcending one's role to behold the possibility of goodness in the other. I left Sale Hall chapel shaken and transformed. And I saw an auditorium full of strong, tough young leaders suddenly wrestling with their value systems and new possibilities for leading change.

Morehouse Mentoring Practices

In the strong culture of Morehouse there were several other practices that contributed to the development of young moral agents and leaders. These practices can be used in any community that is working to support the healthy development of its young people. Among them are *messaging, mapping, measuring, mentoring,* and *ministering.* Monitoring by upperclassman and student services staff encourages accountability and responsibility for one's brother. Although monitoring used to be done through watching academic performance and follow-up personal inquiry, today it is largely done through phone calls and text messages.

The president *messaged* high expectations for us in every speech or conversation. The faculty transmitted knowledge, sharpened our critical thinking skills, and projected vocational possibilities for us, sometimes in ways that were personal and challenging, such as,

"Mr. Jones, you are from Cleveland and could become a future congressman from Ohio. What can you tell us about the protections specified in the Civil Rights Act?"

The faculty members *mapped* possible paths to future service and success. Also, they *measured* our progress as all teachers do when they grade papers and offer evaluative comments. Together, faculty and staff *mentored* us as so many in our ranks were first-generation, low-income students. We needed to see what we could become.

Teachers invited graduates from various professions to visit class to talk about their experiences, their struggles, how they overcame racism and personal failures, and they invited us to become proteges. I became a protege of State Senator Julian Bond, a lifelong dream, along with my classmate Derek Alphran, who went on to become a distinguished constitutional law professor.

There are people who need more than these conventional points of contact, support, and guidance. In the previous chapter I quoted Ernest Hemingway: "Life breaks everyone, but some are made strong in the broken places." Some have not yet been made strong and continue to live with trauma. For those friends and neighbors the college provided exceptional counseling and chaplaincy services for *ministering* to the brokenness. Ministering is the art of healing and shepherding people toward greater wholeness; contentment with themselves; reckoning with the people, places, and things that have broken them; and claiming the agency necessary to move forward.[43]

This Morehouse Mystique has been an inspiration to many families around the nation and world. Unsurprisingly, some of the nation's most influential individuals and families have entrusted their sons to Morehouse. When I retired from Morehouse, I was curious about institutions in other cultures that assumed a similar role in marginal communities. I asked, "Given the remarkable impact that

---

[43] Although we did not see this as a practice, it should be noted that all colleges, particularly small ones, strive to raise and provide money to enable students to persist to graduation.

one small college has had on the trajectory of American democracy, primarily through leadership development, what and where are the 'Morehouses' in other national and cultural locations?"

I mention two of them because they offer lessons for US-based institutions that are attempting to cultivate good citizens and leaders in communities. In Brazil, in the Bahia de Salvador, I was directed to an extraordinary coeducational community center, the Steve Biko Institute, that was working up and down the power structure. That is, its leaders and staff were advocating for increased access to higher and technical education for the Afro-Brazilian population. At the same time they were conducting classes to train teenagers to work effectively in corporate settings. In addition to technical and interpersonal skills, the Steve Biko Institute also emphasized the history of their people, celebrating their agency for struggle and their village values that resist hyper-individualism, materialism, and violence.

In New Zealand, one of the most beautiful countries in the world, I encountered something unique among the indigenous Maori people. Their leaders worried that their young people were yielding to the pressure to assimilate into Western culture and abandoning traditional folkways. In the city of Rotorua, Maori churches are working to inculturate young people with historical values and empowering them to assimilate into the larger society to make their contributions. A language professor developed an app for mobile devices that teaches the Maori language and traditional culture to the next generation. Some versions include games that test vocabulary retention and awards points for correct answers. Participants can trade their points for desirable gifts and personal items. I found this approach to utilizing social media and mobile technology as aids to cultural education a fascinating model for American communities and others around the globe.

Both of these examples illustrate the importance of cross-cultural information sharing and collaboration on best practices for helping marginal and at-risk youth to become proud and productive members of their communities.

My experience at Chautauqua and Morehouse illustrate how *institutions with strong cultures produce strong leaders*. The challenge today is that most American institutions in our diverse and busy society are not very strong. Families, schools, congregations, government at all levels, businesses, and many nonprofits do not appear to have the capacity to withstand the challenges of modernity. I hope and pray that there are many exceptions to what I have observed around the nation, but generally speaking, these foundational or anchor institutions are not cultivating or even encouraging citizens to be virtuous. These institutions lack the authority to inspire virtue. They lack the sense of community capable of inviting and inspiring membership and loyalty.

But this need not be a death knell for institutions that are searching for reinvention. It is time for the renaissance—the rebirth—of those institutions. It is time for convening all stakeholders to begin reimagining their futures. There are skilled organizations and consultants that can assist in this process of reviving or reinventing their identities and missions for the twenty-first century.

4

Can We Repair?

*The greatness of America lies not in being
more enlightened than any other nation, but
rather in her ability to repair her faults.*

—ALEXIS DE TOCQUEVILLE

*It isn't that the evil thing wins—it never
will—but that it doesn't die.*

—JOHN STEINBECK

*Watching you hold your hatred for such a
long time I wonder: Isn't it slippery? Might
you not someday drop it on yourself? I wonder: Where does it sleep if ever? And where
do you deposit it while you feed your children
or sit in the lap of the one who cherishes
you? There is no graceful way to carry hatred.
While hidden it is everywhere.*

—ALICE WALKER

Moral leadership is on the rebound. Social crisis, polarization, fear
and a deeper hunger for a more just society create conditions for
moral leaders to emerge.

Can a nation that is finally beginning to reckon in a more candid way with its original sins (Native American removal and African American enslavement) amid dramatic political, economic, religious and ethnic polarization repair itself?

There are some reasons for hope. And, I hope that each of you will participate in the challenging work ahead of healing and re-building our divided nation.

A 2018 report titled "Hidden Tribes: A Study of America's Hidden Landscape" was produced by an organization called More in Common.[1] The research provides a helpful snapshot of polarization in contemporary America. More in Common is governed by an international board and seeks "to build societies that are stronger, more united, and more resilient to the increasing threats of polarization and social division" by developing and deploying "positive narratives that tell a new story of 'us,' celebrating what we all have in common rather than what divides us, and connecting people on a large scale and across lines of difference, through events and campaigns."[2]

The report identifies seven population segments that seem to "have distinctive sets of characteristics," listed from left to right on the ideological spectrum:

- *Progressive Activists:* younger, highly engaged, secular, cosmopolitan, angry.
- *Traditional Liberals:* older, retired, open to compromise, rational, cautious.
- *Passive Liberals:* unhappy, insecure, distrustful, disillusioned.
- *Politically Disengaged:* young, low income, distrustful, detached, patriotic, conspiratorial.
- *Moderates:* engaged, civic-minded, middle-of-the-road, pessimistic, Protestant.

---

[1] Stephen Hawkins, Daniel Yudkin, Míriam Juan-Torres, and Tim Dixon, *Hidden Tribes: A Study of America's Polarized Landscape,* More in Common website (October 2018).

[2] More in Common website.

- *Traditional Conservatives:* religious, middle class, patriotic, moralistic.
- *Devoted Conservatives:* white, retired, highly engaged, uncompromising, patriotic.[3]

The graphic in the report labels the first group and the last two groups "Wings," and the remaining middle groups "Exhausted Majority."[4]

They suggest that the polarization that we are experiencing is "rooted in something deeper than political opinions and disagreements over policy." Rather, deeper core beliefs are underwriting the polarization. And, on a hopeful note, their evidence suggests "that 77 percent of Americans believe our differences are not so great that we cannot come together."[5]

The approach seems to affirm Aristotle's ancient wisdom about pursuing the golden mean. The report suggests that if we bracket extremists on both ends of the spectrum, Americans are not as far apart as we think. The approach of deploying positive narratives that celebrate actual, not just aspirational, common ground seems promising and reminds me of the suggestions we offered in Chapter 2 on framing issues as moral issues that invite people to join in.

A smaller-scale project brings conservatives and liberals together to better understand each other. This initiative is led by David Blankenhorn, who has also been a strong advocate for strengthening fragile families. Soon after the presidential election of 2016, Blankenhorn contacted me requesting input and endorsement of a new community healing process called Better Angels. What emerged is quite hopeful. In fact, I found its positive narrative to be quite inviting:

---

[3] Hawkins et al., *Hidden Tribes*, 7.
[4] Ibid., 6 (Fig. 0.1).
[5] Ibid., 5.

In December, 2016, 10 Trump supporters and 11 Clinton supporters gathered in South Lebanon, Ohio, in what became the first *Better Angels Red/Blue Workshop*. The goal? To see if we could respectfully disagree and find any common ground. The results were remarkable. We liked each other. We wanted to know more about each other. We wanted to keep on meeting. We wanted to help start workshops in communities all across America! Those reds and blues invited their friends to another workshop and helped to found the first *Better Angels Alliance*.

National Public Radio found out about us and devoted an hour to Better Angels. The word spread, and we started getting emails from people across the country asking, "Can you please come to my community?" We did a summer bus tour, starting in Waynesville, Ohio, and ending in Philadelphia, PA, visiting 15 communities. We followed this with a fall tour starting in Washington, DC, proceeding through North Carolina and ending in Nashville, TN. In addition to holding workshops, we trained 130 volunteers to moderate additional workshops in the future—and the geometric expansion was on![6]

Peter Wehner, senior fellow at the Ethics and Public Policy Center, mentioned Better Angels in a National Review interview: "David Blankenhorn says that the group's goal is 'achieving disagreement.' It's to talk across our differences as fellow citizens."[7]

This medium-scale effort that convenes, fosters dialogue and listening, and promotes relationship building has made an impact on many lives. I hope it will continue to draw more people and train more community-based leaders. Like my class on moral leadership, I hope that the Better Angels approach will also be offered to members of Congress, the White House, and the Supreme Court.

---

[6] "Our Story: How We Started," Better Angels website.

[7] Peter Wehner, "A Political Renewal?" NR interview (June 11, 2019).

The Aspen Institute illustrates another targeted approach by convening people whom it refers to as "weavers." In 2019, "#WeaveThePeople gathered 250 people from around the country who are healing America's social fragmentation by weaving deep connections across difference in their communities."[8] One of the visionaries involved is my long-time friend Eric Liu, who is executive director of the Aspen Institute's Citizenship and American Identity Program. I invited him to speak at Chautauqua Institution, and, as he shared his story of growing up in a Chinese immigrant household in California, he highlighted three dimensions of citizenship: values, systems, and skills.

The values segment focuses on articulating (and updating) an ethical and creedal framework for American civic identity. The systems segment includes policy proposals, cultural initiatives, and multi-sector collaborations to build social cohesion. The skills segment teaches leaders to construct coalitions and a sense of shared fate across increasingly rigid class and race divides.[9]

Below the level of organizations are several friend-to-friend efforts that have gotten traction in recent years. I participated in a wonderful pairing of diverse leaders as part of the Atlanta Friendship Network. The pairings agreed to meet once a quarter for lunch and conversation. Once a year they gather with their spouses. Launched by William G. Nordmark III, CEO of the Nordmark Consulting Group, and John Thomas Grant Jr., former CEO of 100 Black Men of Atlanta, this effort has helped build bridges among the leaders and decision makers in the city. My partner is Rabbi Peter Berg, senior rabbi of the historic Temple in Atlanta. I have

---

[8] Sophia Rivera-SIlverstein and Ben Berliner, "Five Lessons for Changemakers from #WeaveThePeople," The Aspen Institute website (May 17, 2019).

[9] Aspen Institute, "Citizenship and American Identity Program," Aspen Institute website.

learned a great deal from him, and we have helped each other to better understand our shared city. The nearly two hundred couplings of friends continues to flourish despite the heartbreak of Bill Nordmark's sudden death in 2018.

Another pair of friends are attempting to dismantle racism in Christian communities. Teesha Hadra and John Hambrick have published *Black and White: Disrupting Racism One Friendship at a Time*, which tells the story of their determination to tackle America's most difficult moral issue.[10] Their hopeful book has been endorsed by one of Atlanta's most influential pastors and a significant national voice among evangelicals, Andy Stanley. Stanley declares:

> Awareness creates discontent. A lack of awareness often results in complacency. When it comes to racism there's no room for complacency. Especially for Christ followers. In *Black & White* my friends Teesha Hadra and John Hambrick stir our awareness. My hope—their hope—is that having become aware we will become permanently and passionately discontent with racism in all of its insidious forms and expressions.[11]

These and many other initiatives are moving forward and that is good news. But we will again miss a great opportunity unless moral agents and leaders seize the day to enable good impacts from these glimmers of hope and possibility.

We opened this chapter with the compelling words of Alexis de Tocqueville, a French observer of America in the nineteenth century. "The greatness of America lies not in being more enlightened than any other nation, but rather in her ability to repair her faults."[12] What are we to make of this claim?

---

[10] Teesha Hadra and John Hambrick, *Black and White: Disrupting Racism One Friendship at a Time* (Nashville, TN: Abingdon Press, 2019).

[11] Ibid.

[12] Alexis de Tocqueville, *Democracy in America,* vol. 1 (1835), chap. 13.

While leading a class on racial justice and healing in 2019 at the Glenn Memorial United Methodist Church on the Emory University campus, I asked participants to discuss this quotation. Half of them believed that America does possess a special set of qualities and tendencies—pragmatism, hopefulness, inventiveness—that has enabled us to make progress, albeit slowly and often dragging the naysayers forward. The other half decided that de Tocqueville's claim is exaggerated and was not fully true at the time he wrote.

Indeed, his book *Democracy in America* appeared two decades before the Civil War and reminds us that Americans were content to allow the enslavement of other free human persons for over two centuries until moral leaders brought the contradiction to a head.

Almost no one remembers or recognizes the first speech that Dr. King delivered. It was his first or "trial" sermon at Dexter Avenue Baptist Church and was titled "Three Dimensions of a Complete Life." He delivered the sermon numerous times throughout his ministry.

Many more people recognize parts of his first public address in December 1955, the evening after Rosa Parks was arrested. He was called upon to deliver remarks for which he had a half hour to prepare. It was a remarkable oration, as he placed the proposed bus boycott in a long history of protest and movements for freedom. People who listened that night could not have known what they were getting in a national spokesperson. Eight years later they would not have been surprised to hear his "I Have a Dream" speech. The courage, the clear analysis, the emotionally lifting rhetoric, and the driving spiritual determination were by then familiar.

Although that message has proven to be his most iconic, perhaps his most haunting sermon was "I've Been to the Mountaintop," delivered on April 3, 1968, on the evening before his assassination. I have always felt a special connection to this sermon because I knew the venue where he delivered it. It was the headquarters of the Church of God in Christ near downtown Memphis. In November of each year members of the denomination would gather in

Memphis for over a week of worship, meetings, and social life. The building is named after the founder of the church and is known as the Charles Harrison Mason Temple, or just Mason Temple. Sitting in the building in the early 1960s, I used to think that it was the largest building in the world. Years later, history books noted that Dr. King delivered his final speech in a Masonic temple. I would grow angry to read this and would correct our books in class. The teachers were annoyed with me and assumed I did not know what I was talking about. But nearly all of our history books had two photos from the civil rights era, and both of them related to images in my personal life: the grave-side ceremony or interment of Emmett Till, where his mother is shown being consoled by my pastor, Rev. Louis H. Ford, and the image of Mason Temple.

After 1968, whenever I have visited Memphis, I go to stand in that pulpit. I sit in the chairs placed as they were on the night of King's final sermon. This is enough to transport me back to 1968. I look out across the vast sanctuary and imagine a stormy night with rain and thunder. I see King struggling with a headache and a cold. I hear his mellow baritone as he sings a tune that was expected, demanded, by his audience. He could do this effortlessly. He had done it hundreds of times. All speakers and preachers know how to activate the cruise control for a good speech. But that night he surprised many by talking about his inner fears and anxieties in a way that was somehow more foreboding than before. He speculated that he might not be alive much longer. He had deactivated the cruise control and was now transparent. He would be dead by the next afternoon.

1968. As I related in the Preface, that was about the year that my grandmother stormed out of the house to confront two groups of young men, saying, "No one is fighting here today!" There is another piece to that story. Grandma kept a garden right next to her house, the house where my parents and I spent my earliest years. When an abandoned house was torn down, she tilled the soil and cultivated a garden. It was urban creation ex nihilo. I helped pull stones and bricks from the land and watched this woman who had worked the land in Mississippi do her magic on the South Side of Chicago. She grew tomatoes, carrots, lettuce, collard greens, onions, green beans and more. Then she would harvest and prepare fresh meals. That's why she was in the kitchen when the young men were arguing in front of her house. She delivered hot meals to indigent families and to all of the people on the prayer list (the sick and the shut-ins) at church. For some reason she thought that this gave her moral authority—superpowers—to expect goodness in her world. But she also fed the friends of my uncles, who also lived in that house. Many of those men imbibed large quantities of alcohol and managed the challenges they must have encountered every day by drinking at night. They all came to Grandma's house for dinner. Now and then her friends, the church ladies from the Church of God in Christ, dressed in starched white nurses' clothing, and the "winos" would gather on the same front porch to enjoy a southern meal.

As a kid I realized that her house was far more inclusive, welcoming, and affirming than our church, which was led by a young, ambitious male pastor. This was the other side of courageous moral leadership. She gathered people at a common table. She prepared and served them. She loved every one of them. She was called Martha. And when history requisitioned her, she could also run from the kitchen to the streets when violence threatened.

Moral leadership is the highest calling available to human beings. Although we feel barely capable of it, the fact is that we can mobilize integrity, show courage, and summon imagination to serve the common good. We can become more astute students of the moral life, framing issues as moral issues that invite others to act and striving to live exemplary lives while still remaining undaunted by failure. We can invest in enduring institutions and, with grace and courage, we can teach others wisdom, a righteous impatience for the good, and to die with dignity. Women and men who center down, step forth, and dream up for the common good can do anything. Yes, we can—*Sí, se puede!*

Appendix

For Further Reading

As noted above the literature on ethical leadership is expanding. Here are comments on a number of works that have made an impact and especially impressed me.

James McGregor Burns's *Leadership* (1978), a massive study, has become a foundation for all modern leadership studies. His book was the big stone dropped into the pond that generated thousands of waves. He offers a classic distinction between "transactional leaders" who provide goods in exchange for votes, money, or loyalty, and "transformational leaders" who develop mutually uplifting relationships with their followers and "raise one another to higher levels of motivation and morality" beyond "every day wants and needs."[1] There is also John Gardner's "The Moral Aspects of Leadership" (1989), in which he argues that "leaders should serve the basic needs of their constituents," defend "fundamental moral principles," seek the "fulfillment of human possibilities," and improve the communities of which they are a part."[2]

---

[1] Deborah Rhode, ed., *Moral Leadership: The Theory and Practice of Power, Judgment, and Policy* (San Francisco: Jossey Bass, 2006), 6, quoting James McGregor Burns, *Leadership* (New York: Harper Colophon Books, 1978), 36.

[2] John W. Gardner, "The Moral Aspects of Leadership," *National Association of Secondary School Principals Bulletin* 73, no. 513 (January 1, 1989): 43.

Psychiatrist Robert Coles highlights the exemplary lives of several Americans in *Lives of Moral Leadership* (2000).[3] Coles is noteworthy as something of an academic evangelist for moral leadership. He taught the first course, "The Moral Leader," at Harvard Business School in the 1980s. He introduced literature-based learning to Harvard undergraduates and then to all of Harvard's graduate and professional schools—medicine, law, business, divinity, design, architecture, politics. He noted that "novels and stories are renderings of life; they can not only keep us company, but admonish us, point us in new directions, or give us the courage to stay a given course. They can offer us kinsmen, kinswomen, comrades, advisers—offer us other eyes through which we might see, other ears through which we make soundings."[4] More contemporary audiences who viewed the popular series *Game of Thrones* may find Coles's wisdom best summarized in the final episode by the character Tyrion Lannister. "Stories. There is nothing in the world more powerful than a good story. Nothing can stop it. No enemy can defeat it."[5]

Responding to the overwhelmingly masculine-centered content and tone of moral philosophical literature, Cheshire Calhoun of Colby College edited a much needed volume titled *Setting the Moral Compass: Essays by Women Philosophers* (2004) that contains essays by "leading women philosophers in ethics who have contributed to setting the compass in moral philosophy over the past two or three decades." I was especially appreciative of Martha C. Nussbaum's contribution, "The Future of Feminist Liberalism"; UCLA philosophy professor Barbara Herman's essay, "The Scope of Moral Requirement"; and Calhoun's own contribution, "Common Decency."[6]

---

[3] Robert Coles, *Lives of Moral Leadership: Men and Women Who Have Made a Difference* (New York: Random House, 2000).

[4] Robert Coles, quoted in Sandra J. Sucher, *Teaching the Moral Leader* (New York: Routledge, 2007), 11, 12; and *The Moral Leader: Challenges, Insights, and Tools* (New York: Routledge, 2008).

[5] *Game of Thrones*, HBO television series, May 19, 2019.

[6] Cheshire Calhoun, ed., *Setting the Moral Compass: Essays by Women Philosophers* (Oxford: Oxford University Press, 2004), 72–112.

Applying a similar critique about overgeneralizing the moral experience of conforming and comfortable majority males, sociologist Beverlyn Lundy Allen documents the distinctive genius of black female leadership, and offers an important critique of traditional male dominated approaches to leadership theorizing:

> Leadership as a social phenomenon has too often been defined in male terms or associated with elitist positions and operationalized in the "public sphere." Consequently, leadership theories are rarely generalizable to women and minorities.[7]

Deborah L. Rhode's 2006 edited volume *Moral Leadership* (cited in footnote 1) provides the best overview of modern moral leadership literature that I have found. It includes chapters entitled "Morals for Public Officials," "Ethics and Philanthropy," and "Perspective on Global Moral Leadership." In a conversation with the author, she described a forthcoming project that will utilize exemplary biographies of several leaders—including Thurgood Marshall, Ida B. Wells-Barnett, and Mahatma Gandhi—to highlight how virtues and character are formed.

Sandra J. Sucher teaches moral leadership at Harvard Business School. She follows the insights and methods of Robert Coles, which center on biography and literature as portals into the theoretical issues of virtue and justice. In *The Moral Leader: Challenges, Tools and Insights* and its companion volume, *Teaching the Moral Leader: A Literature-based Leadership Course, A Guide for Instructors*, we find chapter-length excerpts from a variety of extraordinary writings, including Chinua Achebe's classic novel *Things Fall Apart* and *Washington Post* publisher Katherine Graham's *Personal History*.

---

[7] Beverlyn Lundy Allen, "Black Female Leadership: A Preliminary Step toward an Alternative Theory," dissertation, Iowa State University (1995), 1. Allen calls for a "reconceptualization of leadership with race, class, gender and cultural inclusiveness" and an insistence on proper documentation of the heroic work on nonelite black women who led movements of cultural resistance for dignity and participation.

Walter Fluker directed the Leadership Center at Morehouse College for many years and subsequently was Martin Luther King Jr. Professor of Social Ethics at Boston University's School of Theology. His book *Ethical Leadership: The Quest for Character, Civility and Community* (2009) has been an important contribution to thinking about character, civility, and community.[8] That work builds on his earlier edited collection, *The Stones That the Builders Rejected: The Development of Ethical Leadership from the Black Church Tradition* (1998). Both texts bring forward the wisdom that has been forged by African American Christians.[9]

Joan Goldsmith and Warren G. Bennis's *Learning to Lead: A Workbook on Becoming a Leader* (2010) is a very practical approach to the self-examination that leaders should undertake as they prepare to step forward to serve.[10] I have used this workbook with students who are new to the vocation of leadership; it walks them through essential questions and issues that can determine their effectiveness as leaders.

David Brooks is one of the nation's most widely known and trusted journalists and social commentators. I was privileged to get to know him at the Chautauqua Institution, and we shared the stage at a Trinity Forum program in Atlanta.[11] His book, *The Road to Character* (2015), is an accessible and engaging survey of the compelling lives of several exemplary people who embody important moral values.[12]

---

[8] Walter Earl Fluker, *Ethical Leadership: The Quest for Character, Civility, and Community* (Minneapolis: Fortress Press, 2009).

[9] Walter Earl Fluker, ed., *The Stones That the Builders Rejected: The Development of Ethical Leadership from the Black Church Tradition* (Harrisburg, PA: Trinity Press International, 1998). The volume contains important essays by Peter J. Paris, Cheryl Townsend Gilkes, Marcia Y. Riggs, Clarice J. Martin, Carolyn C. Denard, and Michael Eric Dyson.

[10] Warren Bennis and Joan Goldsmith, *Learning to Lead: A Workbook on Becoming a Leader* (New York: Basic Books, 2010).

[11] David Brooks and Robert Franklin, "Evening Conversation with David Brooks and Robert Franklin," Character, Civility, and Pluralism series, Trinity Forum, Atlanta, February 21, 2017.

[12] David Brooks, *The Road to Character* (New York: Random House, 2015).

David P. Gushee and Colin Holtz's *Moral Leadership for a Divided Age: Fourteen People Who Dared to Change Our World* (2018) follows a similar method of talking about virtue and ethics through the lens of the lives of a collection of history-making individuals such as William Wilberforce, Harriet Tubman, Elie Wiesel, and Malala Yousafzai.[13] Presidential historian Doris Kearns Goodwin has written a compelling book, *Leadership in Turbulent Times* (2019), about four styles of presidential leadership: transformative (Lincoln), crisis management (Theodore Roosevelt), turn around (FDR), and visionary (Lyndon Johnson).[14]

Many other fine books focus on moral leadership within particular sectors, highlighting exemplars; an example is Richard Zitrin and Carol M. Langford's *The Moral Compass of the American Lawyer: Truth, Justice, Power, and Greed* (1999). There, we find Robert F. Kennedy's extraordinary affirmation of the virtue of courage: "Courage is the most important attribute of a lawyer. It is more important than competence or vision. . . . It can never be delimited, dated, or outworn, and it should pervade the heart, the halls of justice, and the chambers of the mind."[15]

At a time of uncertainty about the future of healthcare in America and pervasive hope for reform with justice, Elvira Nica of the Bucharest University of Economic Studies notes in "Moral Leadership in Health Care Organizations" that "leadership is the most significant component in configuring organizational culture, so guaranteeing the required leadership schemes, conducts and qualities is key to health service enhancement."[16]

---

[13] David P. Gushee and Colin Holtz, *Moral Leadership for a Divided Age: Fourteen People Who Dared to Change Our World* (Grand Rapids, MI: Brazos Press, 2018).

[14] Doris Kearns Goodwin, *Leadership in Turbulent Times* (New York: Simon and Schuster, 2019).

[15] Richard Zitrin and Carol M. Langford, *The Moral Compass of the American Lawyer: Truth, Justice, Power, and Greed* (New York: Ballantine Books, 1999), quotation on 71.

[16] Elvira Nica, "Moral Leadership in Health Care Organizations," *American Journal of Medical Research* 2, no. 2 (2015): 118–123.

F. Stuart Gulley has produced an inspiring volume focused on the life and work of former Emory University president James T. Laney, *The Academic President as Moral Leader* (2001). Gulley presents key insights from the articles, speeches, and sermons by the eloquent and visionary Dr. Laney.[17] In 2011, Laney addressed the International Association of Methodist Schools, Colleges, and Universities. He closed his address with words that provide a moral framework for the work of liberal arts institutions:

> Every year on your campuses students come with various capacities, ambitions, and aspirations. . . . Did you know that you are involved in things that are noble? Books to keep. Grounds to maintain. Buildings to build. Students to bring into the admissions class. But at bottom, if we are not involved in something noble that touches the heart . . . then we have forgotten our vocation.[18]

Earlier in this book I indicated my special respect and appreciation for those who have sat in the hot seat of leadership and later paused to reflect and write about the moral dimensions of leadership. Former FBI Director James Comey has written a compelling account of his time working with President Trump. The book, *A Higher Loyalty: Truth, Lies, and Leadership,* offers a valuable case study for current and future leaders who will face decisional crisis situations where they feel pressure from a person in authority to violate their personal values and may later feel moral injury.[19] Comey has stated that "King's 'Letter from Birmingham Jail' . . .

---

[17] F. Stuart Gulley, *The Academic President as Moral Leader: James T. Laney at Emory University 1977–1993* (Macon, GA: Mercer University Press, 2001).

[18] James T. Laney, "The Education of the Heart: Distinctive Qualities of Methodist Institutions in the Formation of Leaders," keynote address (Washington, DC: International Association of Methodist Schools, Colleges, and Universities, July 24, 2011).

[19] James Comey, *A Higher Loyalty: Truth, Lies, and Leadership* (New York, Flatiron Books, 2018).

is the only book I've read repeatedly as an adult." And a *New York Times* review of Comey's *A Higher Loyalty* comments: "Both his 1982 thesis and this memoir highlight how much Niebuhr's work resonated with him."[20]

Comey concludes his book observing that a morally corrupt administration is similar to a forest fire that does great damage but can also bring growth. "I wrote this book because I hope it will be useful to people living among the flames who are thinking about what comes next. I also hope it will be useful to readers long after the flames are doused, by inspiring them to choose a higher loyalty, to find truth among lies, and to pursue ethical leadership."[21]

Senior diplomats Philip Zelikow and Condoleezza Rice have written *To Build a Better World: Choices to End the Cold War and Create a Global Commonwealth.* They conclude with a question—"Can a confident America Rise Again?"—and underscore the need for leadership that understands and creates the global commonwealth as a moral imperative.[22]

Finally, although there are scores of academy-based programs that focus on moral leadership, and I have written earlier about the unique campus-wide leadership culture at Morehouse College, for some time I have admired the curriculum and priorities of the University of Richmond's Jepson School of Leadership Studies. As its website indicates: "The Jepson approach to leadership ethics rests on the assumption that leadership is a subset of ethics rather than ethics being a subset of leadership studies because a leader/ follower relationship is a moral relationship." This insight echoes that of James McGregor Burns's *Leadership* (1978), quoted at the opening of this chapter.

---

[20] Michiko Kakutani, "James Comey Has a Story to Tell. It's Very Persuasive," *New York Times* Book Review, April 12, 2018.

[21] Comey, *A Higher Loyalty*, 277.

[22] Philip Zelikow and Condoleezza Rice, *To Build a Better World: Choices to End the Cold War and Create a Global Commonwealth* (New York: Twelve Hachette Book Group, 2019).

Index of Names